WRITERS AND CRITICS

Chief Editor
A. NORMAN JEFFARES

Advisory Editors
DAVID DAICHES
C. P. SNOW

ÈNE IONESCO is perhaps the most radical of all the
contemporary dramatists who are trying to revolutionise
our accepted conceptions of the theatre by breaking
away from the realistic traditions of the nineteenth
century. But most Anglo-Saxon audiences are still so
used to the convention of naturalism in the theatre that
many English and American playgoers do not always
find it easy to understand or fully appreciate a dramatist
whose plays may seem to defy the principles of "real"
life. This book (which is the first book about Ionesco
and his work . .t has been published) will therefore be
widely welcomed.

Dr Richard N. Coe is Lecturer in French in the
University of Leeds. He is interested in all aspects of the
theatre, and has also published various works on
Stendhal and on some aspects of the eighteenth century,
together with a number of translations.

13. 785.

13.

IONESCO

RICHARD N. COE

OLIVER AND BOYD

EDINBURGH AND LONDON

OLIVER AND BOYD LTD
Tweeddale Court
Edinburgh 1

39A Welbeck Street
London W. 1

First published 1961

Printed in Great Britain for Oliver and Boyd Ltd
By Robert MacLehose and Co. Ltd, Glasgow

CONTENTS

ACKNOWLEDGMENTS

Thanks are due to M. Eugène Ionesco for permission to reproduce all quotations from his works.

Acknowledgments are due to the following for permission in connexion with the works of M. Ionesco mentioned: John Calder Ltd. (*Plays*); *Evergreen Review* (*Scène à quatre*); and to the following for articles by M. Ionesco: Amis du Théâtre Populaire (article in *Bref*); *Arts*; *L'Avant-Scène*; Cahiers des Saisons; *Cahiers libres de la jeunesse*; Institut International du Théâtre (article in *Théâtre dans le monde*); *Les Lettres françaises*; *Spectacles*; *Théâtre populaire*; *Tulane Drama Review*.

Acknowledgments are also due to the following for permission to quote from the works indicated: *Express* (article by R. Kanters); *Nouvelles littéraires* (article by E. Mora); *Pensée française* (article by G. Lerminier).

The photograph on the front cover is reproduced by permission of Mark Gerson (Photography) Ltd.

R.N.C.

Non era lecito odiare altro
che l'eternità.

Giuseppe Tomasi di Lampedusa

ABBREVIATED TITLES
BY WHICH SOME OF IONESCO'S WORKS
ARE CITED IN THE TEXT

Except where otherwise stated, references by which Ionesco's plays are cited are to one of the collected editions (for full details of which, see below, p. 115). Wherever two references are given together, the second (in brackets) is to *Plays*, tr. Watson and Prouse.

PLAYS

L.S.	=	*Théâtre* (Collection Locus Solus), Vol. I.
N.R.F.	=	*Théâtre* (Collection N.R.F.), Vol. I or Vol. II, as indicated.
Plays	=	Plays, tr. Donald Watson (Vols. I–III) and Derek Prouse (Vol. IV).

ARTICLES AND INTERVIEWS

"D. Th."	=	"Discovering the Theatre."
"E.I.o.f."	=	"Eugène Ionesco ouvre le feu."
"Entretien"	=	"Entretien avec Eugène Ionesco."
"Finalement"	=	"Finalement, je suis pour le classicisme."
"L'Invraisemblable"	=	"L'Invraisemblable, l'insolite, mon univers."

CHAPTER I

THE NEW THEATRE

A "realistic theatre," to all intents and purposes, is a contradiction in terms. The drama is an artistic medium which of necessity is governed by its own laws, and in no case are the laws which determine a form of art identical with those which control the raw material of "real" life. The moment an experience is transferred from life to the stage, it undergoes a radical transformation, and such lingering elements of "realism" as it may retain are nothing but the product of a skilful illusion. More than anything else, it is the realisation of this fact that characterises the *avant-garde* theatre of the twentieth century. The whole art of the theatre is precisely the art of illusion; but to limit the scope and blunt the purpose of this imaginative vision, to restrict it and to curtail it, so that in the end it dare attempt nothing save the photographic reproduction of a specific and small part of the raw material (human "reality") amidst which it was primitively conceived, is "absurd"—a monstrous waste of time and energy, a frittering-away of vital resources, worse (in Ionesco's words), a "distortion," a "shabby piece of trickery,"[1] by which an audience is cheated into believing that there is no "reality," save what may be equated with "realism."

It was as a by-product of eighteenth-century scientific rationalism that the theory of a realistic drama gradually emerged; and conversely, as soon as rationalism began to lose its hold upon the imaginative consciousness of Europe, so creative artists in every field began to cast around for means of expression which should transcend

the narrow bounds of naturalistic representation. But of
all art forms, the theatre has proved the slowest to adapt
itself to such a sweeping revolution—necessarily so, since
its audience is the mass; and whereas a painter can sell
his work and live, if he find but *one* connoisseur both
sensitive and wealthy enough to appreciate him, the
dramatist must count his converts by the thousand before
he (and his dependent actors) can hope to earn a living.
And so, more than half a century after the protests of
Strindberg and Claudel and Jarry, the "naturalistic"
theatre still lingers on in every capital in Europe: in
Moscow, haltingly supported by the doctrine of "socialist
realism" and the memory of Gorky; on Shaftesbury
Avenue (and on Broadway), carefully tended by considerations of box-office; in Paris, reviled and despised
by every critic of repute as "théâtre de boulevard," fit
only for shop-girls, *concierges*, and visiting Anglo-Saxons,
yet prosperous none the less and apparently inexpugnable.

To sort out this confusion between reality and "realism" is the first avowed intention of Ionesco's theatre;
and if he states his case in somewhat sweeping terms, it is
because over and beyond the question of dramatic
technique lie further meanings and more significant
implications:

I have always thought that the truth of fiction is more
profound, more charged with meaning than everyday
reality. Realism, whether it be socialist or not, falls
short of reality. It shrinks it, attenuates it, falsifies it;
it does not take into account our basic truths and our
fundamental obsessions: love, death, astonishment.
It presents man in a reduced and estranged perspective. Truth is in our dreams, in the imagination. . . . [2]

Plainly, there is scarcely a painter or sculptor of importance during the past sixty years who would not fully
subscribe to this doctrine; and significantly, Ionesco—at
one time a friend of Kandinsky—is not merely himself a

connoisseur of abstract painting, but often writes of the theatre, and indeed uses the stage as though it were a canvas. Here, however, the intellectual takes over from the artist, and pushes the platitude neatly over into paradox:

Only myth is true: history, attempting to realise it, disfigures it, half ruins it. History is imposture, mysti-fication, when it claims that it has "succeeded." All that we dream is capable of realisation. Reality, on the other hand, does not have to be capable of realisation: it is only what it is.[3]

Yet, in the paradox, Ionesco is as deeply involved, and just as sincere, as in the platitude. In terms of theatre, the extension of reality means abolishing, not so much the outward manifestations of known and natural behaviour, as the underlying assumptions which are made—sub-consciously and automatically—as soon as we attempt to think *about* the world of daily experience. The prevailing concepts of time and space, of cause and effect, of psycho-logical continuity—these are a few of the preconceived notions in terms of which the rationalistic mind is ac-customed to value and assess "reality." The theatre in particular has been bound to these concepts, since they have always been, even in the centuries before the official formulation of rationalism as a philosophy, the "com-mon-sense" assumptions of the average man—that is, of the average audience:

All the plays that have ever been written, from Ancient Greece to the present day, have never really been any-thing but *thrillers*. Drama's always been realistic and there's always been a detective about. Every play's an investigation brought to a successful conclusion. There's a riddle, and it's solved in the final scene.[4]

It is Choubert, the hero of *Victimes du devoir*, who makes this pronouncement; even the classics, he concludes a

few lines later, are nothing but "refined detective drama
... just like naturalism."[5] But if "realism" and the type
of plot which is based upon the "common-sense" assumptions essential to detective fiction (rational motives,
workable methods, the stimulation of curiosity by the
logically-plausible unfolding of events)—if these things
are not "reality" at all, but merely arbitrary conventions
limiting the true exploration of reality, then the "new
theatre"—Ionesco's theatre—will of necessity be singu-
larly revolutionary in *form*, if not in content: an "irra-
tionalist," a "non-Aristotelian" drama, based on "a
different logic and a different psychology,"[6] in which the
most deep-rooted convictions and beliefs of the "average
man" are flouted with belligerent extravagance.

In his attitude towards the established theatre, Ionesco
is nothing if not belligerent: but occasionally his relent-
less paradoxes, his aggressive *avant-gardisme*, are liable to
do him a disservice. His stress upon his own originality,
upon his lonely "ten-year fight against the bourgeoisie,"[7]
tends to suggest that he occupies an unreal position in the
history of dramatic development. No artist of his stature
stands alone; nor is it conceivable that, together with
Brecht, he should have become one of the two most
widely-performed contemporary dramatists in the world,
unless the ground had been thoroughly prepared before-
hand. No one, moreover, is more willing to admit his
debt to others, when the question specifically arises. None
the less, the misapprehension has gained a foothold; and
by a natural process of compensation, an exaggerated
claim to originality, once detected as such, tends to be
countered by a refusal to allow any real originality, even
where it exists. Ionesco is unquestionably one of the most
original dramatists of the century; but to appreciate the
extent and scope of that originality, it is first essential
to try to define its limits.

In particular, there had existed earlier, not merely a
single and isolated dramatist, but a whole literary and

artistic movement, whose one purpose and intention was precisely to extend the bounds of recognised "reality" in such a way as to define the "complete man," and to include in the definition elements not normally acknowledged as such in a rationalistic interpretation. The Surrealist Movement—a loose term embracing writers as far apart as Guillaume Apollinaire and Roger Vitrac, artists as different in temperament as Picasso and Max Ernst—was probably the most dynamic and far-reaching intellectual revolution since the days when Romanticism was a new discovery, and it is perhaps only now that its full implications are being realised. Yet, characteristically, it left little or no impression on the theatre. A few belated and unsuccessful plays by Tristan Tsara; some influence in the work of Vitrac and Georges Ribemont-Dessaignes; and little else. Here again, the traditional conservatism of theatre-audiences (no less than that of their accredited representatives, the established critics) offered a wall of resistance so impenetrable that the Surrealists themselves scarcely bothered to attack it. The total failure of the Surrealist theatre was anything but unexpected; yet the *avant-garde* of the 'twenties always believed that finally the breach must be made, and the survivors of that great period—among others, Philippe Soupault, André Breton and Benjamin Péret —were not slow to acclaim Ionesco as the latest and finest product of Surrealism.

Ionesco's superficial affinities with Surrealism are obvious to the most casual reader or spectator: the dream-sequences, the monstrous objects that intrude upon the stage, the naturalistic treatment of detail in a fantastic universe—from the boots of the corpse in *Amédée* to the description of Roberte I in *Jacques ou la soumission*:

ROBERT FATHER: She's got hips. . . .
JACQUES MOTHER: All the better to eat you with, my child!

ROBERT FATHER: And then she's got green pimples on a beige skin, red breasts on a mauve ground; a strawberry navel, a tongue in tomato sauce; shoulders of lamb and all the beefsteaks required for the kindest regards. What more do you want?[8]

Yet Ionesco has never been willing to consider himself a Surrealist. "I never belonged to their group," he maintains, "nor did I join the neo-Surrealists, for all that the movement interested me."[9] Although Surrealism was a powerful liberating influence (at the age of seventeen, he was writing poems with "surrealist overtones," under the dual influence of Maeterlinck and Francis Jammes), he was always critical of the ideology behind the manifestations. The surrealist revolution, although it "liberated certain tendencies of the human being which centuries of rationalism had persecuted and suppressed,"[10] none the less failed in that it simply let loose the flood of the subconscious, of "love and dreams," without attempting to control and direct the resulting material. Furthermore, it was too optimistic. Dazzled by the vision of escape into a realm of "total reality," it lost sight, momentarily at least, of the danger and the menace inherent in the human condition. Surrealism achieved the spontaneity which is essential to great art, but it lacked the final degree of *lucidity*.[11] Ionesco, on the other hand, has always had as his objective to achieve a delicate balance between the two:

I believe that . . . a writer must possess a mixture of spontaneity, of subconscious impulses, and of lucidity; a lucidity which is unafraid of whatever the spontaneous imagination may give birth to. If one were to insist upon lucidity as an *a-priori* condition, it is as though one were to dam up the sluice-gates. The waters must be allowed to come flooding out; but *afterwards* comes the sorting, the controlling, the understanding, the selecting.[12]

Surrealism, then, is not a major element in Ionesco's heritage. Parallel with Surrealism, on the other hand, there is another, closely-related movement, whose influence cannot be overestimated: the "Collège de 'Pataphysique," and the writer to whose glory the *'Pataphysiciens* devote their superabundance of enthusiasm, intellect and energy—Alfred Jarry. If Ionesco has always denied any affiliation with the Surrealists, he is proud and honoured to be known as a 'Pataphysician; indeed, he is one of the senior officers of this exotic order, a "Transcendent Satrap," and not a few of his works were first published in the *Cahiers* and *Dossiers* of the Collège.

"'Pataphysics is the science of the realm beyond metaphysics [. . .]. 'Pataphysics lies as far beyond metaphysics as metaphysics lies beyond physics—in one direction or another."[13] The 'pataphysical sciences were discovered (or rather "realised") by Jarry, and the earliest martyrs in the cause were Père Ubu and Dr Faustroll. The Collège, however, was not founded until after the Second World War, by Dr I. L. Sandomir, since when it has developed into one of the most significant "off-beat" intellectual movements that Western Europe has yet produced. Among its Transcendent Satraps are numbered Raymond Queneau, the late Boris Vian, Jacques Prévert, René Clair, and the painter Jean Dubuffet; yet the science is not easy to define. In the words of Roger Shattuck, the "Proveditor-General Propagator for the Islands and the Americas," the very attempt "to define 'Pataphysics in non-'pataphysical terms is a self-contradictory task."[14] To understand 'Pataphysics, however, is half the battle in trying to understand Ionesco; furthermore, to grasp Ionesco's relationship to the Collège is also to grasp his complex relationship as a dramatist with Jarry; and so—even within the limits of this brief study—the "self-contradictory" task must be attempted.

The "science" of 'Pataphysics marks the extreme point of reaction against the physical sciences as such, and against the mentality which they encourage. To exist in a totally deterministic universe, wholly controlled by the laws of cause-and-effect and their consequences, represents an intolerable burden to a certain type of sensitive imagination. The dictatorship of science can be no less oppressive than the dictatorship of Big Brother, and this dictatorship is the more depressing in that it has no logical right to exist. The hypotheses of science are based upon the provisional and tentative conclusions of experiments, and have nothing of the imperative necessity of pure logic. The 'pataphysical attack on science aims straight at the "provisional" quality of experimental evidence. Every phenomenon, according to the 'pataphysicians, is a law unto itself: "'Pataphysics is the science of the particular, of laws governing exceptions". Certain exceptions occur more frequently than others; and it is these—none the less *exceptional* for the comparative frequency of their occurrence—which have been made the subject of scientific generalisations. But "the realm beyond metaphysics will not be reached by vaster and vaster generalities"—because generalities merely finish up by obscuring the value and the reality of the particular. In the 'pataphysical universe, "every event determines a law, a *particular* law"—which is the same as saying that there is no law, neither scientific, nor moral, nor aesthetic. The 'pataphysical doctrine marks an extreme stage of philosophic anarchy; but it is an anarchy of a non-destructive nature, characterised on the one hand by an effervescence of gaiety (cp. Dubuffet), on the other by a broad and universal tolerance: the 'pataphysicians are the latter-day descendants of Pierre Bayle. "For 'Pataphysics, all things are equal"; the "scientific" and the "nonsensical" weigh alike in the scale of eternity, since both are arbitrary, both are absurd. In the scale of *human* values, however, the "nonsensical" is preferable, since it allows greater freedom to the mind of man. "To tell a *comprehensible* tale," writes Jarry, "serves only to oppress the mind and to distort the memory, whereas the absurd exercises the mind and gives the memory work to do."[15] 'Pataphysics rejects the search for truth (a "generality") in favour of a "voyage of discovery and adventure into what Jarry called *ethernity*—which, of course, is where we all live." It seeks for reality in terms of contradiction, it rejects all *a-priori* values. It "preaches no rebellion and no acquiescence, no new morality nor immorality, no political reform nor reaction, and certainly no promise of happiness or unhappiness." Above all, 'Pataphysics incarnates, through its very absurdity, the practical philosophy of the absurd:

> 'Pataphysics has nothing to do with humour or with the kind of tame insanity psychoanalysis has drummed into fashion. Life is, of course, absurd, and it is ludicrous to take it seriously. Only the comic is serious.[16]

To interpret Ionesco in terms of 'Pataphysics is simple; to interpret either in terms of any other concept is exceedingly difficult, precisely because both deal with a human situation from which the element of rationality (and of rational language) is absent. From the dramatic point of view, the essential fact is that, thanks to his contact with the Collège, Ionesco's relationship with Jarry is at once deep and indirect. It is not that he uses the processes, or in any way "imitates" the techniques of *Ubu Roi*, except in so far as his comedy victimises, not the character on the stage, so much as the spectator himself; Ionesco's Jarry is that of *Dr Faustroll* rather than that of *Ubu*; he has lived so much in Jarry and through Jarry, that he can write plays in which Jarry's "influence" counts for nothing, and yet which perfectly reincarnate the total ideal for which Jarry once stood.

This method of approach is very characteristic: Ionesco accepts none of his predecessors at their face value, but absorbs all they have to give him, and rejects the rest. His independence is clearly illustrated in the case

B

of Artaud. Antonin Artaud—half-crank, half-genius—
has become, since his death in 1948, one of the most
fashionable theorists of the *avant-garde*, and, together with
Edward Gordon Craig, is held up as the only true prophet
of the anti-realist theatre. Yet whereas Adamov, for
instance, describes himself as being "nourished upon *The
Theatre and its Double*,"[17] Ionesco is much more cautious
in his approach, and accepts nothing from Artaud, however fashionable, unless it corresponds with his own ideas
and needs. He accepts the notion of Western European
culture as being "corrupt and unauthentic" (that is,
divorced from other aspects of life); he shares Artaud's
passionate belief in a "metaphysical theatre"; he ap-
preciates and develops the principle of "poetry in space"
—*i.e.*, the use of *all* the elements of the stage, and in
particular the *décor*, as active ingredients in the creation
of a "total theatre," instead of subordinating all else to
the spoken word:

> A theatre which subordinates the *mise en scène* and the
> production, *i.e.*, everything in itself that is specifically
> theatrical, to the *text*, is a theatre of idiots, madmen,
> inverts, grammarians, grocers, anti-poets and posi-
> tivists, *i.e.*, Occidentals. . . .[18]

—above all, he accepts the basic notion of "shattering
language in order to reconstitute it anew and to touch
life";[19] none the less, he accuses Artaud of ignorance, of
incompetence in the realm of the practical drama, and of
a kind of insensitive dogmatism which, in the end, is
destined to do more harm than good in the crusade
against the *théâtre de boulevard*.

All these—the Surrealists, the 'Pataphysicians, Jarry,
Artaud—unquestionably did much to make Ionesco
acceptable to the public of today. Yet parallel with his
extremely critical approach towards certain of these predecessors, there exists in Ionesco a curious, almost a
perverse tendency to "invent" ancestors of his own—

dramatists such as the Spaniard Miguel Mihura, or more significantly, the Rumanian Ion-Luca Caragiale, whose contribution to the anti-realist drama was almost nil, yet who are raised to a pinnacle of greatness by virtue of qualities which lie entirely in the eye of the beholder: Ionesco himself.

Caragiale, the "national poet" of Rumania, who is hailed by present-day Marxism as "one of the most implacable enemies of the Rumanian ruling classes,"[20] has been extolled by Ionesco (who is certainly not a Marxist) as "probably the greatest unknown dramatist in the world."[21] Both verdicts are wrong, both are equally subjective. Not that Caragiale is an inconsiderable dramatist, by any manner of means: a social satirist in the traditions of Russian realism, strongly influenced by Ostrovsky and to a lesser extent by Gogol, his plays, in particular *Mr Leonida confronted by the Reaction* (1879) and *A Letter lost* (1884), deserve to be more widely known. To Ionesco, however, Caragiale is already half-Ionesco— or at any rate, half-Beckett: his characters, like those of *End-game*, "are sunken utterly in the irrationality of cretinism"; his language, like that of *La Cantatrice*, is a chaos in which ideas "lose all trace of meaning";[22] his bourgeoisie, like that of *Jacques*, is doomed to ignominious extinction in a morass of metaphysical absurdities. Ionesco's resolve to conjure up for himself a genuine Rumanian "precursor" out of such unpromising material is puzzling; the more so, since there is a much likelier source of inspiration to be had in the works of Demetru Demetrescu-Buzau (1883–1923), who, under the pen-name of Urmuz, not only dominated the Rumanian surrealist movement, but was a fearless pioneer of the absurd.

These, then, are some of the ancestors of the "theatre of the absurd"—the New Theatre which is destined to replace the decaying and irrelevant realism of the bourgeois-scientific tradition. To them, in an infinitely subtler yet still more penetrating way, we should perhaps add Chekhov, the true founder of the "drama of non-communication." But if, to Ionesco, the absurdest incongruity in the modern world is the persistence of "bourgeois realism", this is not only because "realism" is an aesthetic *non sequitur*, but also because the "bourgeoisie" itself constitutes a glaring philosophical anomaly.

To a greater or less degree, all Ionesco's drama is a satire upon the bourgeoisie, its speech, its manners, and its morals, from the *Bouvard-et-Pécuchet*-style parody of *La Cantatrice*, by way of the more specifically social ironies of *Jacques*, *L'Avenir* and *Le Tableau*, to the devastating yet ever-compassionate condemnations of *Amédée* and *Le Tueur*. But from the outset, if we are to grasp Ionesco's implications, it must be appreciated that the terms "bourgeois, bourgeoisie," etc., hold overtones of significance which by far transcend their simple social or political connotations.

If material reality is only a part of total reality; if the freedom of dreams, the illogicality of the subconscious, the terror of nightmare, and the lucid awareness of absurdity, are as much a part of the ultimate truth of being as are science and logic, progress and enlightenment, then to accept only the logical, scientific, and material aspect of existence is to undermine the very dignity of man and to reduce him to the petty dimensions of a marionette. But such is the secret aim and object of "realism" in art; and realism in art being the product of a bourgeois culture, such must, therefore, be the characteristic obsession of the bourgeoisie itself. But man is defined in terms of his obsessions; consequently, whatever society or culture can be shown to prefer the material or the logical or the scientific to the total, uncaused freedom of the irrational is, *ipso facto*, "bourgeois," regardless of its wealth or poverty, its political constitution or its ideology. In fact, even to possess a logical or quasi-logical ideology is in itself "bourgeois," in Ionesco's use of the term; and indeed, "often, alas, the most detestable kind of bourgeois is the anti-bourgeois kind of bourgeois":[23]

From the theatre, as from all present-day writing, the humorous and the absurd have been banished; in their place we find, either a superficial and worldly commercialism, or else the sordid "literature" of commitment. For quite a while now, our whole way of life has been characterised by this lack of humour on the one hand, by the ferocity of "committed" thinking on the other. Hitler had no time for humour; Maurras used to believe that "politics came first"; while the Stalinistic bourgeoisie, whether in Russia or in the West, being devoid of understanding, has forbidden the imagination to be imaginative, that is, to be free, and, in the exercise of its freedom, to be a revealer of truth; *realism* rears its ugly head—a narrow brand of realism, confined to a single plane of truth, so narrow, so distorted by its own fanaticism, that it turns out, in the end, to be a plane of total unreality; and meanwhile we are caught and held in the birdlime of *Sartrisms*, imprisoning us deep in the dungeons and fetters of this "commitment" which should, by rights, be freedom. Each and every one of these "committed" programmes, whether today's or yesterday's, have led, or may still lead, directly into concentration camps set up by the most divergent and contradictory fanaticisms; or else to the institution, both on the intellectual and on the material level, of régimes whose apparent differences serve only to mask their fundamental similarity—their identical domineering bourgeois spirit, with its heaviness, its stupidity, its seriousness, its hatred of fantasy, its "realism," where "realism" signifies a systematised and incomplete conception of a reality which has been falsified and mechanised.[24]

This very broad and quasi-philosophical interpretation of the term "bourgeois" was already current among the German Expressionists as early as 1917, and was propounded, in particular, by Kasimir Edschmid. It explains much in Ionesco's attitude towards the commercial theatre, towards Brecht and Sartre, towards Communism in general; it does not, however, *exhaust* the subject of his political opinions, which, in England at least, have been seriously misinterpreted, and which will be discussed in a later chapter. Nevertheless, on the stage, and in particular on the stage of a non-didactic, uncommitted theatre, such thunderous denunciations of the bourgeois mentality would be badly out of place; instead, Ionesco gives us satire, and with it, a kind of dusty, sordid, hallucinatory poetry, compounded partly of disintegrating platitudes, partly of disintegrating clothes and furniture, the whole being caught up and incarnated in the recurrent figure of the *concierge*, with her meaningless gossip, her intolerable vulgarity, her egoism and her odious alternations of subservience and arrogance: the ultimate and repulsive symbol of a decaying bourgeoisie.

In such a context of meaning, the theatre of Bertolt Brecht must also be accounted a "bourgeois" theatre; but Ionesco's implacable hostility to Brecht (who, after all, was similarly concerned with the destruction of the *théâtre de boulevard*) is complicated by other, more technical, factors: in particular, by Brecht's attitude towards the actor, and by the problem of "*Verfremdung*" ("estrangement").

To Brecht, no less than to Ionesco, it was intolerable that the actor should "create the perfect illusion," for the "perfect illusion" was neither reality nor unreality, neither death nor life, but an "inconceivable" hybrid of the two, whose only outcome was falsehood. Brecht solved the problem by reducing his actors to a wholly subservient role within the machinery of the production, prescribing exactly the degree of "naturalism" with which they should act, and then relying on special effects of the *mise en scène* to shatter the illusion, and to force the audience to "judge" the play as a play rather than to "participate" emotionally in the action. In other words between actor and audience a certain "estrangement" had to be maintained; and this was achieved specifically by the producer, who might manipulate the actor to suit his purpose. For Ionesco, on the other hand (and here the influence of Artaud may be suspected), the essential was to compel the actor to *act*, to act creatively and violently, never creating a "perfect illusion," but rather by the dynamic quality of art, forcing the spectator, against his will and judgment, to participate in an act of imagination which his reason told him was "absurd." Thus, although the primary objective (the shattering of realism) was the same in both cases, the means of achieving it were diametrically opposed. "To nullify the initiative of the actor," protests Ionesco, "is to kill him, is to kill the *life* of the performance."[25] There is yet a further reason, however, why Brechtian methods have proved totally unacceptable to Ionesco. The weakness of any theory of "estrangement" which relies on the *mise en scène* to shatter the illusion, as can be observed in most of Brecht's own plays, in some of Pirandello's (*Tonight we Improvise*), above all in Claudel's experimental *Christophe Colomb*, is that the process of deliberately cutting off the audience from participation in the drama wastes an unconscionable amount of dramatic time, with the result that the content of the play needs to be drastically stripped, simplified, etiolated—and the emotions sentimentalised. With Ionesco, however, from the first, dramatic *density* has proved a primary requirement (perhaps no French writer since Molière has achieved so much in each scene); and so to the clash of personalities and ideologies is added the clash of methods.

Rather than build up a semi-realistic illusion and then shatter it, Ionesco's method is to start with an unrealistic —preferably an impossible, an inconceivable—situation, and then to develop it, still "impossibly" and "inconceivably," as far as it will go, yet at the same time forcing the audience to participate in what is not an "illusion of reality," needing a recurrent and clumsy shattering, but indeed *total reality* itself, in all its nightmarish and contradictory absurdity. As a clue to Ionesco's basic concept of the drama—as opposed to Brecht's—there is a striking passage in the essay, *Discovering the Theatre*:

I can still remember that as a child my mother could not get me away from the puppet-shows in the Luxembourg Gardens. I could have stayed there spellbound for days on end. I didn't laugh, though. The spectacle of the *guignol* held me there, stupefied by the sight of these puppets who spoke, who moved, who bludgeoned each other. It was the spectacle of life itself which, strange, improbable, but truer than truth itself, was being presented to me in an infinitely simplified and caricatured form, as though to underline the grotesque and brutal truth.[26]

This tendency to write for living actors as though for marionettes is fundamental to Ionesco's vision of the New Theatre: the use of grotesque masks in *Jacques* and in *L'Avenir*, the macabre and burlesque elements in *Amédée* and *La Leçon*, the constant stress on the "enlarging of effects," by means of which everything is "pushed to a state of paroxysm, there where the sources of tragedy lie"[27]—above all, the detailed acting instructions given at the head of *Le Tableau*—show clearly how far Ionesco draws upon the "clownish" techniques of the puppet and marionette theatres, and also of the circus, in order to achieve his "return to the intolerable," to a theatre "which attains to probability by dint of improbability and *idiocy*."[28] It is significant that these same preoccupations with caricature, grotesque hallucination, and nightmare, appear as early as 1945, in the introduction to a translation of Pavel Dan's *Le Père Urcan*, long before Ionesco had ever dreamed of turning towards the drama as a means of expression. This suggests—and the suggestion is confirmed at every step—that Ionesco's basic dramatic technique, far from being a mere means for attaining certain specific effects, reflects an integral part of his vision of the universe. If the actor's art is to be based upon that of puppets and marionettes, it is because the actual world in which we live is first and foremost "a world of the *guignol*."

As to the actual significance of the New Theatre, Ionesco has written almost inexhaustibly. He has even contrived to introduce large chunks of theorising into the plays themselves; not merely in *L'Impromptu de l'Alma*, which is a dramatised satirical essay, but even in *Victimes du devoir*:

NICOLAS D'EU: Inspiring me with a different logic and a different psychology, I should introduce contradiction where there is no contradiction, and no contradiction where there is what common sense usually calls contradiction. . . . We'll get rid of the principle of identity and unity of character and let movement and dynamic psychology take its place. . . . We are not ourselves. . . . Personality doesn't exist.[29]

But these elliptically provocative statements have been illustrated and amplified since in a score of explanatory articles. At the basis of Ionesco's concept of the New Theatre we find over and over again the notion of *freedom*. "The very act of creation," he asserts, "presupposes *total freedom*";[30] political freedom, of course, as a *sine qua non*; but beyond that, an aesthetic freedom which it is perhaps still more difficult for the dramatist to achieve—a freedom to explore, to accept whatever revelations may be vouchsafed in the actual experience of writing, consequently freedom from any form of *a-priori* concept, whether ideological, or whether simply related to a specific notion of psychology or art. Ionesco's plays tend to grow in total freedom out of themselves: "invariably, I find in myself that it is some primary image, some initial rejoinder, which sets off the whole mechanism of creation [. . .]. I never know exactly where I am going."[31] Obviously, however, there are difficulties inherent in such a process. To accept without prejudice whatever aspect of reality, nightmarish, clownish, or horrific, may arise from the act of creation, without clamping down with some form of subconscious *a-priori* judgment, *and yet to remain basically lucid*, implies the attainment of a state of 'pataphysical "imperviousness" which, in fact, can be attained only through humour: hence the dictum, "Humour *is* liberty."[32] Comedy, therefore, is an essential factor, not merely in Ionesco's outlook, but in his actual creative method; he could not create otherwise than humorously, for, by the terms of his own definition, without humour he would not be free to create at all.

The outcome of such a process must, at first, appear arbitrary; art would seem to be anything that the merest accident might cause to swim into the dramatist's awareness. Yet, in practice, this is not the case; the imaginary might *seem* to be anarchic, but in fact it "is bound by its own laws,"[33] and these laws are the laws of "ultimate reality." Ionesco's theatre, in other words, is nothing but "the projection on to the stage of the world within";[34] a world which is part of the reality of "universal experience," a world whose sole and unique justification and *raison d'être* is "its own existence."[35] Thus the theatre, which is the revelation of this world, itself requires no other justification for its existence than the fact, simply, that it *is*. The logical conclusion of this argument is the unfashionable dogma of "Art for Art's Sake"; and Ionesco has no qualms whatsoever about drawing it:

The artist is not a pedagogue, nor is he a demagogue. Dramatic creativity fulfils a need of the spirit; this need must be sufficient unto itself. A tree is a tree [. . .].

A tree is not concerned to present itself in more comprehensible form; if it did, it would no longer be a
tree. It would be the explanation of a tree. Similarly,
the work of art exists in its own right, and I can quite
readily conceive a theatre without an audience. . . .[36]

This last quotation brings us back once more to the
fundamental problems of realism, but this time points
towards a far more radical solution. For if, in order to
portray the "universal nature" of reality, the theatre
must be "totally free," it is not enough for it merely to
divest itself of *a-priori* aesthetics, ideologies and psychological behaviour-patterns. All these, in fact, would
vanish of their own accord, could the drama once escape
the fundamental confines of materiality. To some extent,
the fetters of material realism may be loosened by such
techniques as have already been suggested; but not wholly
so. The material image, and hence the temptation of
"representation" and of "dramatic illusion," is always
present to some extent, inevitably. Or is it so? If it were
possible to create an *abstract* drama, as wholly non-representational as abstract painting, a dramatic equivalent of
a Klee or a Kandinsky, then, but only then, would total
freedom be in sight. And this, in fact, is Ionesco's
ultimate ambition:

As plots are never interesting, it is my dream to rediscover the rhythms of drama in their purest state, and
to reproduce them in the form of pure scenic movement. I should like to be able to create an abstract, a
non-representational theatre. How is one to set about
it?[37]

The answer—or half of it at least—is supplied by
Ionesco himself at the beginning of the quotation, when
he talks of the "rhythms of drama in their purest state."
Stripped of its representational elements—plot, logic,
realism, and all the trappings of the "detective" school—
Ionesco's theatre, if it is to hold together at all, must

discover new sources, both of unity and of dynamic tension. And the nature of these sources has already been indicated: on the one hand, the use of *rhythm* pure and simple as a primary factor in dramatic structure; on the other, the persistence of unresolved *antagonisms*.

At the root of these antagonisms lies the fundamental conflict between the comic and the tragic, producing the "tragic farce," which is the specific definition given to *La Leçon*, but which might apply equally well to the whole of Ionesco's drama. To emphasise this underlying conflict, however, Ionesco resorts to various other "dynamic opposites": the contrast between the pathetic and the sordid in *Les Chaises*; between the prosaic and the poetic, the surrealist and the banal in *Jacques*; between abstract rhetoric and violent action in *Victimes du devoir*; between the realistic and the fantastic in *Amédée*; between the platitudinous and the impossible in *La Cantatrice*—the effect of all of which is to produce a series of shocks as "dramatic" as any provided by Mr Eric Ambler. But above all, it is the contradiction inherent in the function of the actor himself which is exploited to the full by Ionesco. The fact that the actor is both himself—a banal, existing creature of flesh and blood, with a suburban maisonette, a double-bed and income-tax worries—and at the same time the hero or villain in and through whom he lives, is in itself a flagrant antagonism which, consciously and deliberately exploited, can create a degree of dramatic tension rivalling that of the most lurid of thrillers.

Added to this are the rhythmic patterns of language and structure. An artificial rhythm of dialogue and movement is one of the characteristic devices of farce. But in the tragic farce, the rhythm, instead of being merely comic, takes on a quality of brutality, senselessness, and menace. The rhythm of jazz, the menacing, machine-like vibrations of the twentieth century, underlie all Ionesco's language; unlike those of Ann Jellicoe in *The Sport of my Mad Mother*, his characters supply their own percussion band. Not merely, however, are isolated scenes conceived in this inherently rhythmic manner, but, in the majority of instances, the whole play is constructed round a consciously rhythmic structure. In *La Leçon*, for instance, the "suspense" is that of a purely formal piece of music, and the script could—in fact, should—be marked for tempo like a score. In some of the shorter plays—as in Labiche— the rhythmic qualities of language and structure are deliberately underlined by a balletic pattern of movement: in *Scène à quatre*, Dupont and Durand continually "pace round the table, their hands behind their backs . . . they meet, collide, about-face and move in opposite directions";[38] while in *Le Nouveau Locataire*, as the Removal-Men start bringing in the furniture, "the rhythm, scarcely emphasised, must none the less impart to the action a vaguely *ceremonial* character."[39] More often, however, the tension is provided by subtle variations in speed, in density, even in lighting—witness the almost imperceptible variations in tempo which characterise the various invisible personages of *Les Chaises*, or the carefully-graded progressions of *Le Tueur*.

The nearest that Ionesco has yet come to a purely abstract form of drama was in the *Sept Petits Sketches* of 1953. *Tueur sans gages* and *Rhinocéros* seemed to suggest that the attempt had been abandoned, but even here, there were odd scenes (notably the beginning of Act II of *Le Tueur*) which were curiously choreographic in conception. Inevitably, Ionesco's drama seems to be moving towards the ballet; the stylised gyrations of the Lovers (*Le Maître*) lead directly to the scenario of *Apprendre à marcher*. Yet, in the end, the ballet is not an answer. Even more than music, the ballet, as an art, lacks intellectual density, and Ionesco has far too much to say to accept such limitations. The final resolution of the problem lies still in the future; but there are signs in *Les Salutations*, for instance, or in *Scène à quatre*, of a new direction: a sort of frenzied, rhythmic pattern of words and movement together, neither play, nor ballet, nor burlesque, but a fusion of the three, in which the nightmarish disintegration of intellect is in itself an intellectually forceful assertion.

REFERENCES

1. "D. Th.," p. 3.
2. *Ibid.*
3. *Op. cit.*, p. 4.
4. N.R.F., i. 179 (ii. 269).
5. N.R.F., i. 180 (ii. 270).
6. N.R.F., i. 219 (ii. 308).
7. "Depuis dix ans . . . ," p. 5.
8. N.R.F., i. 104 (i. 132).
9. Reported by Edith Mora, "Ionesco: 'Le Rire? . . .' "
10. "D. Th.," p. 17.
11. E. Mora, *loc. cit.*
12. *Ibid.*
13. *Evergreen Review*, iv, No. 13 ("What is 'Pataphysics."), p. 131.
14. *Op. cit.*, p. 27.
15. Quoted in M. Beigbeder, *Le Théâtre en France depuis la liberation*, Paris 1959, pp. 34–5.
16. *Evergreen Review* (above, n. 13), pp. 27–9.
17. Arthur Adamov, *Théâtre*, Paris 1953–5, ii. 9.
18. Antonin Artaud, *The Theatre and its Double*, New York 1958, p. 41.
19. "Ni un dieu, ni un démon,"

pp. 133–4; cp. Artaud, *op. cit.*, p. 13.
20. Ion-Luca Caragiale, *Théâtre choisi*, Bucharest 1953, i. 8.
21. "Caragiale: 1852–1912," p. 218.
22. *Op. cit.*, pp. 218–19.
23. "Depuis dix ans . . . ," p. 5.
24. "La Démystification par l'humour noir," p. 5.
25. "D. Th.", p. 5.
26. *Op. cit.*, p. 6.
27. *Op. cit.*, p. 10.
28. *Le Tableau*, p. 5.
29. N.R.F., i. 219–20 (ii. 308).
30. "Finalement," p. 1.
31. N.R.F., ii. 13 (iii. 112).
32. "E.I.o.f.," p. 188.
33. *Ibid.*
34. N.R.F., ii. 57 (iii. p. 150).
35. "Le Cœur n'est pas sur la main," p. 264.
36. "E.I.o.f.," pp. 181, 184.
37. "L'Invraisemblable," p. 1.
38. *Scène à quatre*, p. 46.
39. N.R.F., ii. 175 (ii. 241: Watson, however, omits this passage in the stage directions).

CHAPTER II

A WORLD OF INFINITE COINCIDENCE

Realism in art, as we have seen, is inseparable from rationalism; and rationalism itself, in its early stages, was inseparable from the growth of science. For the nineteenth century, all three concepts went hand in hand: every effect was known to have a rationally ascertainable cause, and the existence of an inescapable, deterministic relationship between "cause" and "effect" was one of the fundamental assumptions of Western philosophy. Whatever existed, existed therefore *rationally* and *necessarily*; and, in consequence, art, whose logic was assumed merely to be a by-product of the logic of science and mathematics, could have no higher ambition than to portray, in a medium governed by its own laws, events and objects as they existed in the outside world.

The dissolution of this rationalistically-conceived vision of the universe was mainly due to an instinctive revolt of the spirit of man, which refused to submit to its imprisonment in so confining a cell of material determinism. But it was also due in part to the progress of science itself. Even before the end of the century, there were major writers (such as Dostoevsky and Rimbaud) and minor ones (such as Edward Lear and Lewis Carroll) whose concept of the nature of man either simply failed to be contained within the bounds of rationality, or else preferred to side-step them altogether, and to seek refuge (as did W. S. Gilbert) in a world of mock-logic and childish fantasy. Such figures, however, might have been dismissed eventually as mere eccentrics, were it not for the fact that men of science, shortly afterwards, were heard to be making statements which pointed—or at least, to the layman, appeared to point—in the same direction. Microphysics suggested that certain forms of energy shared simultaneously the contradictory properties of waves and of particles; quantum physics gave it to be understood that the "logically" impossible could and did happen; atomic physics produced evidence which implied that effects need have no necessary cause, and that phenomena might create themselves out of nothing; while Einstein at one blow appeared to invalidate both Euclid and the rational conceptions of time and space. The *exact* significance of these various discoveries, whether to the scientist or to the professional logician, is irrelevant; what matters here is the impression that they left upon the consciousness of the average intellectual or artist. And this impression was one of a major revolution striking at the very foundations of logical thought, and backed by those who hitherto had been the stoutest pillars of rationalism: the scientists. Materialism was not so much "disproved," as ceased imperceptibly to have any particular meaning, since the rational intelligence could no longer even pretend to grasp what "matter" might be; similarly, if "determinism" was discarded, its philosophical significance was undermined, not through the emergence of any rival doctrine, but rather by the realisation that the time-honoured methods of Aristotelian logic, on which it was based, seemed quite incompetent to deal with the type of proposition which was now being put before them.

In a word, it became evident—evident to the artists, evident even to certain logicians of a neo-Hegelian persuasion—that whatever laws the universe was governed by, it was by laws infinitely more subtle and complex than those of classical logic, and consequently that "realism," far from portraying the "only true and necessary" picture of existence, was in fact depicting a positive falsehood. The reaction was immediate: all that had, for the better part of two centuries, been oppressed by the dictatorship of rationalism, came bursting to the surface, and the first half of the twentieth century is a seething mass of cults and movements—Cubists, Futurists, Vorticists, Surrealists, Expressionists, Imaginists, Dadaists, Existentialists—all of them in their own way trying to elucidate the situation of the human spirit in a universe from which logic now seems conspicuously absent.

But in a world from which logic is absent, the "necessary justification" of existence which depended upon logic is similarly missing. In Ionesco, as in Camus or as in Sartre's *La Nausée*, the fact of existence is neither logical nor justified. It is simply a fact; and existence without rational justification is, in the technical language of Existentialism, simply "absurd." "Absurdity," therefore, is a force to be reckoned with—*the* force, indeed, since the so-called determinism of the nineteenth century depended upon an illusion of causality which, faced with the evidence of unresolved and unresolvable contradictions, became suddenly meaningless. The notion of an "absurd," a purely gratuitous universe, is neither an easy nor a comforting one to grasp; it is pleasanter to believe in final causes and Newtonian universal laws. But Ionesco, no less than Camus, is a man obsessed with truth, for whom the "comfortable lie" is anathema. To continue—still, at this late date—to propound the illusion of rationality would be an act of flagrant immorality. To the serious artist, all art is fundamentally moral; and consequently, to Ionesco, the illusions of "naturalism" are not merely invalid, but, on the plane of art and ethics alike, empty, negative, and evil.

The enemies of Aristotelian logic—from Hegel, Engels and the Marxists down to Korzybski and Stéphane Lupasco (the last of these the friend and philosophic mentor of Ionesco himself)—have invariably based their arguments upon the "principle of contradiction." Aris-

c

totle maintains that if you say something, and then deny that very same thing, and go on maintaining both the denial and the affirmation, then you have said *nothing*. But if, argues Lupasco in *Logique et contradiction* (not wholly aware, perhaps, that "contradictory" in logic means what logicians have made it mean, and that it is part of the *definition* of "contradictory" that two contradictory propositions cannot be true—in other words, that the "law of contradiction" is not a law about the non-linguistic world at all)—*if* science or mathematics provides evidence (as it does) of two contradictory statements being true simultaneously, without one of them being *ipso facto* non-existent, then a new logic, or even an anti-logic, is needed to accommodate this fact. Modern research, asserts Lupasco, has revealed to us an inconceivably varied field of experience, whose phenomena engender and organise "a complex and clearly dialectical pattern of relationships." None the less, there is one deep-seated law which seems to control and to formulate these relationships, and by so doing, to define the intrinsic logical structure of the very notion of dialectic: the law of "an antagonistic dualism." In other words, now that science has revealed, not merely intrinsic oppositions or the clash of contraries, but inherent contradictions in its own basic assumptions, it would be a fatal error merely to try to explain them away. It is the old concept of logic, and not the new concept of science, which is at fault; and these unwelcome contradictions in themselves are capable of generating a "dynamism" which promises a renewal of the whole of human thought and experience, aesthetic as well as scientific.[1]

A full analysis of Lupasco is, unfortunately, out of the question in this brief study; were it possible, it would leave little else to be explained about Ionesco's "anti-logic." *Logique et contradiction* ramifies into all parts of experience, from the theories of knowledge and probability to emotion, aesthetics and morbid psychology. To illustrate the deep and constant affinity between the philosopher and the dramatist, one parallel must suffice. "Identity," asserts Lupasco,

> cannot possibly be that which, for all too long, it has been believed to be: something static. Identity is dynamic, and with a dynamism contradictory to the dynamism of diversity, which is thus better defined as *diversification*, just as identity is better defined as *identification*.[2]

If it were necessary to attempt to define, in one philosophical sentence, Ionesco's attitude towards his dramatic characters, it would be difficult to put it more appositely or more succinctly. "I'm all for contradiction," observes the Author in *L'Impromptu de l'Alma*, "everything is nothing but contradiction";[3] and indeed, the whole of Ionesco's world is one in which the carefully-constructed illusion of human logic crumbles hopelessly beneath the impact of this one small but unanswerable factor. Mrs Smith, in *La Cantatrice*, describing a female of the Bobby Watson clan, sets her forth unblushingly as having

> regular features, but you can't call her beautiful. She's too tall and too well-built. Her features are rather irregular, but everyone calls her beautiful. A trifle too short and too slight, perhaps. She teaches singing.[4]

One such assertion is sufficient; logic is destroyed, and nothing is left but an endless series of causeless and unrelated phenomena: a world of infinite coincidence.

In such a world, there is no such thing as familiarity, no such thing as experience, and consequently no valid inductive method of argument. Attempts to reach a workable conclusion by induction, in a context where no experience is *in any way* related to the next, lead to the most ludicrous absurdities—as for instance in *La Cantatrice*, where the Smiths and the Martins debate the possible significance of a ring at the doorbell.[5] Each and every phenomenon, being utterly isolated and un-caused, holds all the qualities of surprise and utter novelty, from the Old Man in *Les Chaises*, who has been told the same bed-time story every night for seventy-five years, and whose memory is still "virgin-new again every evening,"[6] to Bérenger who, both in *Le Tueur* and in *Rhinocéros*, stands constantly dazed with wonder at the beauty and the evil, at the very *fact* of existence. On the other hand, the discovery that every phenomenon is totally unpredictable, and therefore totally surprising, means that there is no real distinction between the utterly fantastic and the unspeakably banal. If Mrs Martin in *La Cantatrice* is bowled over in speechless amazement by the sight of a man bending down in the street to tie up his shoelace,[7] by contrast, both Madeleine and Amédée accept the presence of their macabre tenant in the bedroom with total equanimity and resignation.[8] In other words, even in man's attitude towards the absurd, there are two contradictory forces at work: the absurdity of each indivi-dual phenomenon, on the one hand, which makes the act of reading the newspaper in the *Métro* into a nine-days' wonder; and, on the other, the total absurdity of exis-tence, which reduces the transmutation of man into rhinoceros to the level of a commonplace:

No happening, no particular magic holds any surprise for me, no sequence of ideas can compel my attention, nothing is capable of seeming to me in any way more improbable than anything else, for everything is brought down to the same level, everything is drowned in the general improbability and unlikelihood of the universe itself. The fact of existence, the very use of language—these are what seem to me to be incon-ceivable. Those who have no sense of the absurdity of existence may perchance discover, within the frame-work of this existence, that this thing or that thing may be isolatedly meaningful or logical, right or wrong.

To me, however, it is existence itself that seems un-imaginable; and that being so, there is nothing *within* existence that has the power to startle my credulity.[9]

Two provinces especially would seem to belong by right to the domain of rational man: language and mathematics. It is therefore significant that, in *La Leçon*, these are precisely the two subjects by means of which the Professor brings about the final moral disintegration of his pupil. The question of language will be discussed in the next chapter; as for mathematics, it is fascinating to compare Ionesco's heroes with Orwell's Winston Smith. For the latter, freedom was

The freedom to say that two plus two make four. If that is granted, all else follows.[10]

Winston Smith and Bérenger have much in common; yet for Bérenger (and still more so for the Girl-Student in *La Leçon*) freedom—total freedom—lay in the discovery that two plus two did *not* necessarily make four: a discovery that was terrifying and (likewise for Dany in *Le Tueur*) ultimately fatal, since it meant abandoning the sweet, imprisoning security of reason for a universe of limitless and intolerable absurdity. Not, however, that the moral became immediately apparent: the ultimate significance of the Professor's suave announcement, "In this world of ours, Mademoiselle, one can never be sure of anything,"[11] is not finally revealed until the time of Bérenger's last, most cataclysmic dialogue with the Killer. For mathematics is the very keystone of ration-ality, and where it fails—as fail it must in a universe of coincidence where "seven and one make eight . . . and sometimes nine"[12]—everything else necessarily fails with it, and mankind is swept up willy-nilly, like Amédée, into the night-sky of absurdity, still trailing pathetic little wisps of logic from his ankles:

AMÉDÉE: I'm terribly sorry. Please forgive me, Ladies

and Gentlemen. . . . Please don't think. . . . I should
like to stay . . . stay with my feet on the ground. . . .
It's against my will. . . . I don't want to get carried
away. . . . I'm all for progress, I like to be of use to
my fellow-men. . . . I believe in social realism [. . .].
I swear to you that I'm all against dissolution. . . .
I stand for immanence, I'm against transcendence
. . . yet I wanted, I wanted to take the weight of the
world on my shoulders. . . . I apologize, Ladies 'n
Gentlemen, I apologize profusely.[13]

Ionesco's attitude towards the absurd has not been
wholly consistent; in fact, since *La Cantatrice*, it has
evolved quite significantly, and this very evolution has
dictated a corresponding evolution of dramatic form. At
the outset, the temptation was to counter the illusion of
logic by a kind of dialectic of anti-logic, a dense and
carefully-dovetailed sequence of *non sequiturs*, false syl-
logisms, deductive and inductive arguments divorced
equally from valid first principles and from any relevant
evidence, a pattern of false analogies, arbitrary conclusions, incongruous associations, transferred causalities,
irrelevancies, anomalies, anachronisms, and plain impos-
sibilities, forming a sort of looking-glass universe which is
the direct opposite of that with which we are normally
familiar. This is the stuff of which *La Cantatrice* is made,
likewise *La Nièce-épouse, Le Salon de l'automobile*, and, to a
lesser degree, *La Leçon*. But the danger of this (largely
verbal) irrationalism is that, in the end, it is scarcely less
systematic, or "automatic," than the standard logic of
rationalism. Ionesco's ultimate objective is not to propound a system of illogic which is merely the denial, the
mirror-counterpart of common logic, but to describe a
reality in which the dictates of cause-and-effect are super-
seded by the comparative freedom of an untrammelled
imagination. "Fantasy," he observes, "is a *method of knowledge*: all that is imaginary is true; nothing is true unless it

be imaginary."[14] But the true "imagination" is not so much the antithesis of reason as such, as of an "automatic dialectic" derived from rationalism. The "anti-logic" of *La Cantatrice*, therefore, was far too rigid, was itself far too dense with anti-logical dialectic, to be pursued further; and in later plays we find Ionesco moving steadily away from the artificiality of such brilliant contrivances, towards the less striking, but ultimately more effective "dream-sequences" of *Victimes du devoir* or of *Tueur sans gages*. For the dream-sequence is not, in itself, *anti*-logical; it is merely a series of more-or-less normal events, from which the arbitrary restraint of causality has been removed.

Thus, despite its superb achievement, both as a comedy and as an argument, *La Cantatrice* was to prove a dead-end—just as Adamov's first play, *La Parodie*, was to prove a dead-end, and for similar reasons. Not that the techniques of pure anti-logic are discarded altogether; but when they reappear (as, for instance, in the scenes with the Logician in *Rhinocéros*), it is in a highly simplified, schematised form, usually in combination with some other dramatic device; they tend to be employed rather as means to an end, more and more rarely as ends valid in themselves. What has remained, however, from this "orgy of counter-rational dialectic" (to use Marcel Brion's phrase),[15] has been a supreme contempt for those major conditioning factors of a rational concept of the universe—time and space, the law of gravity and the standard properties of three-dimensional objects.

From its first beginnings, the drama has been at war with itself over the properties of time and space, owing to the need to compress these "real" dimensions into the stylised dimensions of the stage. From Racine's conscientious juggling with the unities to Adamov's "quasi-poetic no-man's-land," where clocks have outsize dials and no hands, the problem has remained essentially similar and essentially unsolved. Given this preoccupation, it is hardly surprising that recent philosophical speculation concerning the fundamental meaning of time—Uspensky, J. W. Dunne, etc.—should have awoken an immediate echo in the theatre. The 'thirties, in fact, saw a whole spate of plays on the subject, from *Space-Time Inn* to *Thunder Rock*; and it is significant that even so firm-rooted a realist as J. B. Priestley—a realist, like M. Botard, "with all four feet on the ground"[16]—should have felt tempted to experiment with time in his plays in a manner that is completely foreign to him as a novelist.

The *avant-garde* theatre has grown to be, almost by definition, timeless: a drama of broken watches. Beckett's tramps, Pinter's caretaker, Adamov's employee (*La Parodie*), no less than Ionesco's Bérenger, live in a world where all the clocks have stopped—and are deeply, almost pathologically, disconcerted by the fact. In *La Cantatrice*, time, like all other significant manifestations of apparent logic, is not merely erratic ("The clock strikes twenty-nine"),[17] but positively perverse:

THE FIREMAN: . . . it depends what time it is.
MRS SMITH: We can never tell the time here at home.
THE FIREMAN: But the clock?
MR SMITH: It doesn't work properly. It's of a contrary turn of mind. It always strikes the contrary to the right time.[18]

Similarly, in *Le Nouveau Locataire*, this wordless tragedy of inanimate encroachment would hardly be complete without its pair of symbolically "gigantic" timepieces.

The logical outcome of a world in which time has shed its comforting assurance of continuity, is that human *age* is meaningless and arbitrary. To Bérenger in *Tueur sans Gages*, his age at any given moment is determined by exclusively emotional considerations: "I could be sixty years old, seventy, eighty, a hundred and twenty, how do I know? [. . .] Time is above all subjective";[19] while the Mother of *La Jeune Fille à marier*, having first asserted that her nubile daughter is ninety-three, then adds that, of course, "she owes us eighty years, so that makes her only thirteen."[20] Furthermore, in a world of infinite coincidence, there is no conceivable "accumulation of experience" related to the passage of years. Old age is just a senseless, arbitrary, unjustified *fact*, devoid alike of honour, dignity or wisdom (*Les Chaises*), and the weight of the past, like so much unmentionable and utterly valueless rubbish, merely clutters up the living-space of the present. "All those wasted years," moans Madeleine to Amédée, "they're a dead weight . . . always with us."[21] The past, in Ionesco's world, has merely the status of an object, a senseless *something* in three-dimensional space. On the other hand, the laws of space itself are equally arbitrary. The Removal-Men in *Le Nouveau Locataire* "bark their shins" on a plain chalk circle drawn upon the floor, and struggle, panting and sweating, beneath the "intolerable burden" of minute and insignificant objects. The Stout Gentleman, in *Le Tableau*, is tirelessly persevering in his efforts to set a three-dimensional crown upon the head of a two-dimensional painted queen. Light streams across the stage in the last act of *Le Tueur*—but *not* from the setting sun, which is shown, opaque and tarnished, on the backcloth. In a world without logic, mankind experiences something of the brutal and terrifying freedom from the conventions of materiality that is said to be experienced by spacemen in the gravity-free confinement of their rocket.

If all apparently "logical" sequences of events, then, are in fact purely arbitrary juxtapositions of unrelated phenomena, the most forceful evidence of this will necessarily be in the human personality itself. A "personality," in the classical concept of the term, implies at least a minimum of continuity from one moment to the next, and not merely an unrelated sequence of "states of existence" accidentally confined within the same material body. But this minimum of continuity is precisely what is lacking. Each "state of existence" owes nothing but an arbitrary debt of coincidence to the one before it. The famous scene between Mr and Mrs Martin in *La Cantatrice* is not merely comedy of the highest order, it is a significant illustration of the "dialectic of the absurd." A married couple of long standing may appear at first sight to possess a kind of joint personality, or at least so deep a knowledge of each other that their lives are to all intents and purposes inseparable. But this stability of relationship is based, in the final analysis, upon memory; and (given the discontinuity of human experience) not even upon the memory of *events*, but, in Bérenger's words, upon "the memory of a memory, like a thought grown foreign to me, like a tale told by another."[22] There is, there can be, no memory of a distant past, nor even of a comparatively recent past, but at best the memory of a similarly "remembered" memory in an immediately preceding moment of existence. At worst, nothing—total amnesia, as in the case of Mr and Mrs Martin, in consequence of which the ultimately coincidental nature of reality appears in its true colours:

MR MARTIN: I have a flat on the fifth floor, flat Number 8, dear lady.

MRS MARTIN: How very extraordinary! Oh goodness gracious, how very amazing and what a strange coincidence! I too live on the fifth floor, Sir, in flat Number 8!

MR MARTIN [*thoughtfully*]: How very extraordinary, how very extraordinary, how very extraordinary, and what a strange coincidence . . .[23]

This characteristic amnesia, revealing as it does the arbitrary quality of all sense-perceptions, is a fundamental theme in Ionesco's drama; the plight of Mr and Mrs Martin is echoed by that of Amédée and Madeleine, who have totally "forgotten" how the Corpse first made its appearance in their bedroom, by that of Bérenger struggling to recall his past beatitude (*Tueur*, Act I), above all by that of Choubert (*Victimes du devoir*), who finishes up in pathetic desperation munching crusts of bread "to plug the gaps in his memory."[24] But this is only half the problem; for if the illusion of "personality" is based upon the merely arbitrary juxtaposition of states of being, there is no self-evident reason why this juxtaposition should be confined within the limits of one particular human aware-ness. Dramatically, this implies the total disintegration of the classical concept of character of the standard defini-tions of psychology. Personalities merge, fuse, exchange, sort themselves out clearly for an instant, only to fuse and merge again—the Concierge graduates imperceptibly into La Mère Pipe (who is a man), while the Architect turns into the Commissaire de Police and later into the Second Policeman (*Le Tueur*). Relationships evolve in the strangest of permutations and combinations: the Marquis incurs the wrath of the law by aspiring to promote his own wife to the status of niece (*La Nièce-épouse*), and the Fireman's tale (in *La Cantatrice*) loses itself in a veritable labyrinth of consanguinities. A single character will pro-liferate into an infinite series of mirror-images of himself: the three Bartholoméuses (*L'Impromptu*), the duplicate Roberte (*Jacques, L'Avenir*), the countless Bobby Watsons, male and female, young and old, married and widowed —but *all* commercial travellers (*La Cantatrice*). Madeleine (in *Victimes du devoir*) mutates opaquely through a whole pattern of personalities: middle-class housewife, erotic *femme fatale*, sharp-tongued shrew and withered hag. Edouard is the double of Bérenger (*Le Tueur*), and they share one set of keys between them. Or else identical scenes repeat, with different "characters" speaking the same lines (*La Cantatrice, L'Impromptu, Rhinocéros*). Nor is there any psychological continuity betrayed by speech. In almost all Ionesco's plays—but above all, in *La Cantatrice*, in *Jacques*, in *Victimes du devoir*, and in the *Sept Petits Sketches*—almost any speech might belong by right to any character—or rather, we are startlingly made aware that the words which we are forced to associate with the speaker of them in fact belong categorically to someone else, to another character on the stage, to some invisible being in the wings, to an animal (cat or rhinoceros), or for that matter to the author himself. Nowhere does Ionesco go further in his contempt for the realist convention than in this total and perfectly lucid, deliberate destruction of the whole dramatic concept of classical "psychology."

On the other hand, the mere "destruction" of character is no more Ionesco's definitive objective than is the simple reversal of accepted logic. The negative antitheatre phase began with *La Cantatrice* and ended with the *Sept Petits Sketches*. His final aim is much more positive: to create a living vision of "reality" sufficiently broad to encompass rational and irrational at the same time. And the only source of such reality is the imagination: more especially, one particular manifestation of imaginative experience, which is the *dream*.

Ionesco (again, like Adamov) freely admits the dream-origin of many of his plays.[25] So also did the Surrealists and, to a lesser degree, the Expressionists. But the Surrealists simply re-experienced through art the inner contents of their dreams, whereas the Expressionists crystallised the dream-elements into sharp-edged, abstract symbols. Too little lucidity on the one hand, according to Ionesco, too much on the other. A careful balance is required, and this can only be achieved by understanding the relationship between dream and waking. The dream is not the means of exploring a world *divorced* from waking reality; it is a means of discovering truths *about* waking reality which must otherwise remain shrouded and hidden:

When I dream, I have no impression of renouncing thought. On the contrary, I have the impression of being able, in my dreams, to perceive truths, whose quality of self-evidence appears to me in a more blinding light than in the waking state [. . .] when frequently everything seems blurred, uniform and impersonal.[26]

In this sense, then, there is no conflict between dream and reality; the dream is "an extension of reality," a "creative act of discovery about reality";[27] the limited reality of the material world is contained within the broader reality of the dream, and not *vice versa*. It is this concept—absolutely fundamental to Ionesco's inner vision—that accounts for the apparent paradoxes of *Le Tueur*: "reality, *unlike dreams*, can turn into a nightmare";[28] and again: "Mirages . . . there's nothing more *real* than a mirage."[29] On the other hand, ultimate reality (the dream), seen in terms of limited reality (the waking state), may often *appear* as nightmare, owing to its very quality of illogic, for man is afraid of nothing so much as of the unfamiliar. Yet, if the full impact of dream-reality is to be appreciated, this fear must be faced—and conquered; for it is only in terms of the "lucid" reality of wakefulness that the significance of the dream can be evaluated. "The psycho-analysis of a nightmare," comments Professor Gouhier, "is a nightmare in itself."[30] And in this sense, Ionesco's vision *is* that of a nightmare world: unreason, viewed from the point of view of reason, yet known to be greater than reason itself, is a terrifying spectacle.

This concept of irrationality has plainly many affinities with that of Kafka—with the Kafka of *Metamorphosis* even more, perhaps, than with the Kafka of *The Trial* and *The Castle*—and the comparison between the two writers has frequently been drawn. In particular, the characteristic "distortion of reality," which is common to both, may be said to serve the same purpose in either case: the unreal is a device for attaining a deeper insight into reality itself. "Distortion," wrote Gunther Anders, "is a device which should be familiar to us all: modern science, in order to probe the nature of reality, places the object of its investigation in artificial, *i.e.*, experimental conditions. This situation distorts nature, and thereby distorts the object; yet the result is a closer approximation to the truth."[31] This verdict on Kafka is not a whit less true of Ionesco: the "dream-distortion" of his work is a laboratory experiment made in the course of a quest for universal truth. Hence Ionesco's contention that his plays are at one and the same time both "scientific" and "classical"—a claim which even his Anglo-Saxon critics are beginning to admit is perhaps not so far-fetched as at first it may sound, since the first part has been admitted by William Saroyan and the second by Lawrence Kitchin.

Pessimism, too, is a factor in common to both the playwright and the novelist. Yet, if both are concerned with the fate of man in a universe from which the "rules"—that comforting semblance of logic and justice—have been removed, there is none the less a difference of emphasis. For Kafka, the sense of man's inadequacy face to face with the absurd finds release in an overwhelming consciousness of guilt. For Ionesco, the guilt is present likewise, in Choubert, in Amédée, even in Bérenger; yet in the end, it is outweighed by an emotion still more overwhelming—the consciousness of *freedom* in itself. In the absence of logic, the freedom of man is literally infinite; but infinity in any form lies outside the range of man's capacity, and so his freedom is not joy, but anguish—an anguish so intolerable that he is forced to celebrate his immersion in the absurd with an absurdity, if possible, still greater: the careful and deliberate invention of a pattern of logic to reign where none exists, which he needs and must acquire if he is to preserve his sanity.

REFERENCES

1. Stéphane Lupasco, *Logique et Contradiction*, Paris 1947, pp. viii–ix and *passim*.
2. *Op. cit.*, p. 22.
3. N.R.F., II. 19 (III. 118).
4. N.R.F., I. 20–1 (I. 89).
5. N.R.F., I. 33–8 (I. 100–5).
6. N.R.F., I. 129 (I. 42).
7. N.R.F., I. 32–3 (I. 98–9).
8. N.R.F., I. 256 (II. 178).
9. "L'Invraisemblable," p. 1.
10. George Orwell, *Nineteen Eighty-Four*, Penguin edn., London 1959, p. 68.
11. N.R.F., I. 60 (I. 7).
12. N.R.F., I. 64–5 (I. 11).
13. N.R.F., I. 320 (II. 225).
14. "La Démystification par l'humour noir," pp. 5–6.
15. Marcel Brion, "Sur Ionesco," pp. 274–5.
16. *Rhinocéros*, p. 158 (*Plays*, IV. 63).
17. N.R.F., I. 28 (I. 96).
18. N.R.F., I. 45 (I. 112).
19. N.R.F., II. 69 (III. 15).
20. N.R.F., II. 255–6 (III. 159).
21. N.R.F., I. 270 (II. 191).
22. N.R.F., II. 80 (III. 25).
23. N.R.F., I. 27 (I. 95).
24. N.R.F., I. 217 (II. 306).
25. Article signed "A.S.," in *Combat*, 26 Feb. 1959.
26. "Entretien," p. 12.
27. "Depuis dix ans . . . ," p. 5.
28. N.R.F., II. 80 (III. 26).
29. N.R.F., II. 72 (III. 18).
30. Henri Gouhier, "Eugène Ionesco," p. 179.
31. Gunther Anders, *Franz Kafka*, London 1960, p. 9.

CHAPTER III

THE APOTHEOSIS OF THE PLATITUDE

The "Drama of the Absurd" was given to the world by France. It is, however, both striking and suggestive that so many of those dramatists who constitute the present-day *avant-garde* hailed originally from abroad. Beckett was born in Dublin, Ionesco in Slatina, Adamov in Kislovodsk; Arrabal is from Spain, Schéhadé from the Lebanon; Tardieu and Pinget are Swiss, while Ghelderode is a Belgian. Despite their diverse origins, all these writers are, in the deepest sense of the word, French; yet obviously their attitude towards the idiom in which they have chosen to write can never be identical with that of the ordinary Frenchman who knows no language other than his mother-tongue. In cases such as these, the style is not, and cannot be, the whole man; part of the man will necessarily remain outside, and judge. And characteristically, with Ionesco, this objectivity, this slight detachment, this minute but ineradicable alienation of thought and language, has developed into a primary element in his philosophy. Language itself is an intrinsic manifestation of the absurd.

In the traditional theatre, language represented a means to an end. It was a means of communication between stage and audience, a means by which various more or less objective concepts were conveyed to the mind of the spectator. These concepts might be derived from the "psychology" of the characters in a given situation, or else related more directly to the "message" of the dramatist himself; they might be largely intellectual, as in Racine, or sensually evocative, as in Shake speare: but in all these cases, the language of the drama itself fulfilled only a secondary function. It might incarnate a character, embody an idea, transmit and intensify an image: but, save in the rarest of poetic instances, and then only for a few lines at a time, it could not *replace* characterisation, or override its own intellectual content, or act as substitute for an image which it might enhance, but could not do without.

Even Antonin Artaud did not finally discard this traditional concept of language. Artaud was concerned to reduce the "literary content" of the drama in the interests of "total theatre"—in other words, finding the Western theatre, in contrast with the dramatic arts of Mexico and of the Far East, effete, abstract, and over-intellectualised, infinitely weakened in its potential impact on the audience by the preponderant role which had gradually come to be usurped by the text, he insisted that language should be evicted from its place of supremacy in the drama. Dramatic speech, he asserted, was merely one means among a number of others (action, gesture, *décor*, costume, lighting, etc), by which an overall theatrical effect might be attained; and to attain that effect with a maximum of violence and intensity, the traditional status of language must be thoroughly humbled.

To some extent, Ionesco answers the demands of Artaud. There are passages—characteristically, at the end of *La Cantatrice* and again in the concluding scene of *L'Avenir*—where language is used almost physically, as a kind of bludgeon or blunt instrument, where in fact the border-line between word and gesture is almost erased, where the spectator is, to all intents and purposes, physically assaulted by the barrage of quasi-meaningless sounds emitted by the characters on the stage:

MRS MARTIN: You cacklegobblers! You gobblecacklers!
MR MARTIN: Cat's lick and pot's luck!

D

MRS SMITH: Krishnawallop, Krishnawallop, Krishnawallop!

MR SMITH: The Pope's eloped! The Pope's no soap!
Soap is dope!

MRS MARTIN: Bazaar, Baseball, Bassoon!

MR MARTIN: Business! Bosnia! Buster!

MR SMITH: Aeiou, aeiou, aeiou!

MRS MARTIN: Bcdfg, lmnpq, rstvwxz!

MR MARTIN: Do re mi fa sol la si do!

MRS MARTIN: Said the barley to the cabbage, said the
cabbage to the oats!

MRS SMITH [*imitating a train*]: Puff Puff Puff Puff Puff
Puff Puff Puff Puff Puff Puff Puff Puff!¹

In this type of passage, language is used, no longer to
make the spectator think, but to provoke him, to force
him, by the sheer violence of sound in a pre-linguistic
state, to react, and to react no less forcibly and decisively
than a man who has been jabbed with a red-hot poker.

But Ionesco goes beyond this point. Artaud's concept
of "total theatricality" still leaves language in its original
secondary role. Even when finally stripped and gutted of
its intellectual content, it is still a means to convey a
dramatic effect which is not inherent in the words themselves, but, in the last resort, alien to them. To make a
drama—or part of one, at least—out of language itself is
to add a new dimension to the theatre; and this is what,
each in his own characteristic manner, Beckett and
Ionesco have attempted.

Vladimir and Estragon, in *Waiting for Godot*, have
nothing to say to each other; they symbolise nothing, they
define themselves neither by their acts nor by their
passions; they are *created* by the language they use, and,
realising this, they talk incessantly, lest, the supply of
words eventually failing, they should cease to exist
altogether. Similarly Krapp, in *Krapp's last Tape*, has
abdicated as an existing being; his whole reality is

usurped by the sound of words which issue from his tape-recorder. In Beckett, human relationships, human existence even, is shown as a function of language; in Ionesco, language not merely creates existence, but, having done so, proceeds to tyrannise and victimise its own creation.

That language can create existence is seen most clearly in *Les Chaises*, where some two-and-thirty creatures of flesh and blood and unmistakable materiality are conjured up, literally out of nothingness, by the words and gestures of the two decrepit caretakers. That language can destroy is seen most vividly in *La Leçon*, where the unhappy Girl-Student disintegrates stage by stage before our eyes beneath the sheer weight and impact of meaningless syllables, and is finally stabbed to death with the word "knife." But these are, in one sense, crude examples. The use of language for the deliberate creation or destruction of others is, comparatively speaking, a rare and insignificant phenomenon beside the experience of words creating or destroying their own utterer. It is not the old, familiar Pirandellian theme of man's failure to express his meaning; rather it is that, in the absence of meaning, the words themselves take absolute control, and drive their unfortunate victim whithersoever their blind and dangerous energies may choose to direct. On different levels, the love-making of Jacques and Roberte II (*Jacques ou La Soumission*), the ravings of the Concierge (*Le Nouveau Locataire*), the poisonous political vituperation of La Mère Pipe (*Tueur sans gages*) and the final transformation of Dudard into an armour-plated perissodactyl (*Rhinocéros*) are all illustrations of mankind victimised by language.

Technically speaking, Ionesco has raised language from the status of a secondary medium to the dignity of an object-in-itself. It does not exist to serve the characters; the characters are simply a vehicle—and a fragile, highly expendable one at that—by which language is conveyed to the awareness of the audience. In certain circumstances, a tape-recorder would do as well. Jean Vannier, in a brilliant article, "Langages de l'avant-garde," has defined the whole of Ionesco's theatre as "a drama of language, wherein human speech is put on exhibition."[2] But since it is language itself which is on display—or, better still, on trial—*nothing* can be taken for granted. Speech, having no a-priori *raison d'être* in the psychology or ideology of the speaker, is forced to pass, phrase by phrase and word by word, through a process of the minutest scrutiny—and more often than not is found wanting and condemned. Thus we get the paradox that Ionesco, having elevated language to an unprecedented height of responsibility in the drama, is at the same time tempted to destroy it utterly; and in this paradox resides the fullest significance of the term "anti-theatre." Language as an object—a proliferating, senseless object, like the coffee-cups in *Victimes du devoir* or the noses on the face of Roberte II—is absurd, is the supreme absurdity; but in a universe of absurdity, that object which is in itself more inherently absurd than any other is the force which rules, the crushing and destructive agent which decides the destiny of man.

André Breton once defined the poet's first duty as that of "stirring up language to a new state of effervescence." In this sense, Ionesco is a true poet, for his final objective is the reconstitution of a new language in which poetry—even the most traditional, "poetic" type of poetry—can once again be written. By showing up the meaninglessness of conventional idiom, by shattering the hard and crystallised phraseology of common speech, his achievement is to throw back into the melting-pot all those individual elements of which rational language is composed; and from there, a whole vocabulary can then emerge anew, scoured of its accumulated patina of overtones and associations: the long-awaited raw material for a new generation of poets to work upon. His humour is like a pick-axe, chipping away persistently at layer after solid layer of fossilised verbal deposits.

For the purpose of demonstrating in dramatic terms the absurdity of language, Ionesco's favourite weapon is the platitude. Certain plays, or scenes within plays, are made up almost entirely, line by abject line, of clichés, slogans, and conversational commonplaces—the cadaveric language of an alienated society. *La Cantatrice*, *Jacques*, *L'Avenir*, *La Jeune Fille à marier*, *Le Maître*, together with the episodes with the Concierge in *Amédée*, *Le Nouveau Locataire* and *Le Tueur*—each in its own way is a study of the "bourgeoisie" (in Ionesco's sense) betrayed and finally annihilated by the hollow and repetitive conformism of its own jargon. Ionesco himself describes the origins and the implications of this necromantic obsession with the carcasses of words in a remarkable passage where he tells how he came to be a playwright:

In 1948, before writing my first play, *La Cantatrice chauve*, I had no intentions of becoming a dramatist. My sole ambition was to learn English [. . .] and so, with this end in view, I slipped out one day, some eight or ten years ago now, and bought a French-English conversational handbook for beginners [specifically, the *Méthode assimil*]. I settled down to work. Conscientiously I set to, and copied out from my handbook lists of "conversational phrases," in order to learn them by heart. But as soon as I came to read them through, I found myself learning, not English, but a series of startling truths: that there are seven days in the week, for instance (which, incidentally, I knew already); or that the floor is *below*, whereas the ceiling is *above*—another phenomenon of which I was basically aware, perhaps, but which I had never seriously reflected upon, or else had simply gone and forgotten, and which now appeared to me, suddenly, as a blinding revelation: astounding, and yet indisputably *true*.[3]

Ionesco's phrase-book introduced him, in successive lessons, to Mr and Mrs Smith (a typical English middle-class couple), to their maid Mary, and finally to their old friends, Mr and Mrs Martin; and amid this typically English group, a series of typically homely English conversations took place:

It was at this point that I experienced a revelation. My aim was no longer to perfect my knowledge of English; a new and broader ambition had taken its place, namely, to communicate to my fellow-men those fundamental truths which had been brought to my awareness by my French-English conversational handbook....[4]

Somehow or other, almost of their own volition, the phrases began to arrange themselves in dramatic form: but as they did so, a weird, a most disturbing kind of dislocation took place; the oddest distortions intervened, the whole of "reality" seemed to disintegrate, and poor Ionesco, from time to time, was forced to go and lie down on the nearest sofa, "trembling with fear lest it should suddenly vanish into nothingness, and myself with it."[5]

This sense of terror at the first revealing contact with the absurd corresponds almost point for point with that of Roquentin in *La Nausée*; but the further conclusions which Ionesco draws from the experience are significantly different from those of Sartre. *La Cantatrice*, he explains, is a vision of

a kind of universal petty-bourgeoisie, the "petty-bourgeois" being the very incarnation of the common-place, of the slogan, of *conformism*, wherever and whenever it occurs; and of course, it is by the *automatism of his language* that the inherent conformism of the bourgeois is betrayed. The text of *La Cantatrice chauve*, or rather, of my handbook of English (or Russian, for that matter, or Portuguese) Conversation, being made up, as it was, of ready-made expressions, of the most threadbare platitudes imaginable, revealed to me, by this very fact, the secret of "talking and saying nothing," the secret of talking and saying nothing *because there is nothing personal to say*, the absence of any inner life, the mechanical soullessness of daily routine: man totally absorbed in his social context and indistinguishable from it. The Smiths and the Martins have forgotten how to talk because they have forgotten how to think; and they have forgotten how to think *because they have forgotten the meaning of emotion, because they are devoid of passions*; they have forgotten how to *be*, and therefore they can "become" anyone, anything, for, since they *are* not in themselves, they are nothing but other people, they belong to an *impersonal* world, they are interchangeable.[6]

This remarkable passage, which not merely explains *La Cantatrice*, but does much to elucidate the whole "problem" of Ionesco, shows clearly that the platitude has not one, but a multitude of functions. On the one hand, as it stands, it is the symbol of all that Ionesco understands by the term "bourgeoisie"—that aspect of humanity which accepts and cultivates the illusion of material realism as being the equivalent of the whole of reality, which renounces the perception of "total reality" (the "inner life") and prefers the superficial comfort of rational logic as displayed in the visible forms of social order; which is therefore hollow within and encrusted without, and in consequence, elementally *stupid*—and elementally *comic*. In this sense, the platitude is a weapon of social and political satire, as well as of philosophical criticism of the human condition. Man has signed his abdication; within, there resides a void, a nothingness, to be filled by words and slogans, until the slogan becomes the whole man, transforming Mr Smith, at the whim of fate, at one moment into Mr Martin, at the next into an "ideologist," a Nazi, a Brechtian, a sectarian dictator, a rhinoceros, a "master of the concentration camps."

But the platitude is not merely revealing; it has also to be revealed. In other terms, nothing is achieved by merely enunciating a commonplace unless, by its very method of enunciation, its essential commonplaceness is made apparent. And this brings us back again to the critique of language. The essence of the platitude is that it is both spoken and listened to, without any immediate awareness of its meaning (or lack of meaning) being present in the mind of either speaker or hearer. Ionesco's problem is that somehow the phrase whose very essence is meaningless insignificance should become significant without thereby becoming meaningful. It must visibly destroy itself, reveal its own absurdity. Thus Ionesco's platitudes are more than simple commonplaces; they are commonplaces which *compel the attention*. They proliferate for page after page, and startle by their very mass:

GENTLEMAN: You could even go so far as to say that civilisation's constantly developing, and in the right direction, thanks to the united effort of all the nations....

LADY: Perfectly true. I was just about to say the same thing.

GENTLEMAN: We've come a long way since the days of our ancestors, who used to live in caves and gobble each other up, and feed on sheepskins! ... What a long way we've come!

LADY: Yes, we have, haven't we? ... And central heating, Monsieur, what about central heating? Did they have that in their caves?

GENTLEMAN: Well now, dear lady, when I was a small child....

LADY: Such a pretty age!

GENTLEMAN: . . . I used to live in the country. I remember it was still the sun that kept us warm, winter and summer alike. We used to light our homes with oil—it's true it wasn't so clear in those days—and sometimes even with candles! . . .

LADY: That happens even today, when the electricity fails.

GENTLEMAN: Machines are not perfect either. They were invented by man and they've all *his* faults!

LADY: Don't talk to me about the faults of men! Oh la la! I know all about that, they're no better than the women, they're all alike, nothing to choose between them.

GENTLEMAN: Of course. So why expect a man to do a job even a machine can't do . . . ?

LADY: I admit I'd never even thought of that . . . yes, when you really come to think of it, it's possible after all, why not?

GENTLEMAN: You see, Madame, mankind's future's in the future. It's just the opposite for animals and plants. . . .[7]

Ionesco's platitudes contradict each other; they invert themselves, garble themselves; they spoonerise, they slip mysteriously out of gear; they harbour grotesque distortions and baroque neologisms ("plauvre, chronométrable, mononstre");[8] they echo proverbs, maintaining sound and discarding sense: "Celui qui vole aujourd'hui un œuf, demain volera un bœuf" contorts itself into "Celui qui vend aujourd'hui un bœuf, demain aura un œuf";[9] while "the rules of the game" becomes "the game of the rules." Occasionally (but rarely) these very distortions harbour a point of satire, but to insist upon a satirical content to the platitudes would rob Ionesco's argument of its main contention: the utter pointlessness of a language which has degenerated into formulæ, whose acceptance, by those who utter them, is symbolic of an inner abdication, of submission to an order "which is defined exclusively by its own slogans."[10]

Ionesco's platitudes destroy themselves, issue forth to battle armed with their own *reductio ad absurdum*. What is missing is a standard of comparison. The inherent absurdity of Molière's grotesques is made apparent by the sober and strictly rational behaviour of the *honnête homme*; but Ionesco has no *honnête homme* to offer. Even Bérenger is a drunkard. In other words, between "meaningful" and "meaningless" there is no sharp distinction; to draw such a distinction, it would be necessary to criticise the platitude in terms of some other category of speech. But there is no other category. Ionesco never identifies himself completely with any of his characters, even when those characters appear to utter his own thought; he never (as a dramatist) accepts implicitly the claim of any language to transmit a thought exactly and without distortion. His position—even in moments of utter seriousness—is always, to some extent, that of the "outsider"; between thought and word there is invariably that imperceptible but unbridged gap. Across this gap, the living energy of meaning cannot pass; and therefore language, even when it imitates almost to perfection the forms it would adopt were life really in it, is none the less dead—one more inanimate object in the world of inanimate absurdity. "Words fall like stones, like corpses"[11] is a characteristic definition, and one which Ionesco has employed more than once. And being dead, words can communicate nothing; for the only alternative to a dead language is, not a living language (there is no such thing), but—silence.

And so the failure of language leads us into a kind of Realm of Terror; again, the science-fiction cliché seems appropriate: the terror of the silence of Outer Space. Ionesco's plays are conflicts between sound and silence, in which silence, in the end, always wins. The New

Tenant, imprisoned for ever in the soundless dungeon of his own furniture; the deaf-and-dumb Announcer of *Les Chaises*; the gradual faltering of Bérenger's impassioned dialectic beneath the shadow of the Killer's knife—all lead by devious routes to the final eclipse of human speech in the last act of *Rhinocéros*:

> BÉRENGER [*fresh trumpetings, hectic racings, clouds of dust*]:
> I can't bear the sound of them any longer, I'm going to put cotton wool in my ears. [. . .] The only solution is to convince them—but convince them of what? Are the changes reversible, that's the point? Are they reversible? It would be a labour of Hercules, far beyond me. And in any case, to convince them, you'd have to talk to them. And to talk to them, I'd have to learn their language. Or they'd have to learn mine. But what language do I speak? What is my language? Am I talking French? Yes, it must be French. But what is French? I can call it French if I want to, and nobody can say it isn't— I'm the only one who speaks it. What am I saying? Do *I* understand what I'm saying? Do I?[12]

Bérenger's plight is that of Man: condemned by the breakdown of language to solitude and silence.

On the other hand, even the physical ability to utter sounds—sentences, paragraphs even—is no real guarantee of communication. All the words in the world, if these words are not specifically related to some object or concept, will not break the fearful silence. And this precisely is the significance of the Professor's "course in comparative linguistics" in *La Leçon*, no less than that of the hallucinating love-scene at the end of *Jacques*. According to the Professor, all languages are identical, and "each single concept is expressed by one and the same word and its synonyms, in all countries of the world";[13] according to Roberte II, all words in any given language are identical:

ROBERTE II: Below stairs in my country house, every-
    thing is puss. . . .

JACQUES: Everything is puss.

ROBERTE II: One name for every single thing: puss.
    The cats are called puss; food, puss; insects, puss;
    chairs, puss; you, puss; me, puss; the roof, puss;
    number one, puss; number two, puss; three, puss;
    twenty, puss; thirty, puss; all the adverbs, puss; all
    the prepositions, puss. It makes talking so easy. . . .

JACQUES: To say: let's go to sleep, darling . . .

ROBERTE II: Puss, puss.

JACQUES: To say: I'm very sleepy, let's go to sleep . . .

ROBERTE II: Puss, puss, puss, puss.

JACQUES: To say: bring me some cold spaghetti, some
    warm lemonade, and no coffee . . .

ROBERTE II: Puss, puss, puss, puss, puss, puss, puss, puss.

JACQUES: And Jacques, and Roberte?

ROBERTE II: Puss, puss.[14]

Jacques and Roberte II, realising the inevitable defeat
of language by silence, the inevitable failure of communication, have given up; but here the terror breaks in
again, because, by giving the same *name* to all things, by
admitting that the verbal symbols for objects are merely
dead sounds, and therefore not worth distinguishing
between, the distinction between *objects* is similarly
obliterated, and the whole familiar universe of common
things is at one stroke reduced to a terrifying facelessness.
The would-be suicide of *La Cantatrice* fails to distinguish
between a gas-oven and a comb;[15] the Customer in *Le
Salon de l'automobile* attributes identical sexual properties
to his car and to the young lady who is selling it to him,
and is quite prepared to marry either,[16] while *La Jeune
Fille à marier* (a nubile wench if ever there was, in her
mother's opinion) turns out to be a strapping young
guardsman with a handlebar moustache. The victimisa-
tion of man by language is now complete; the death of

language has plunged man dizzying backwards, not merely into everlasting silence, but into primeval chaos, where all things are confounded in obscurity.

In such a context, it stands to reason that communication between individuals is "exceedingly difficult," if not, strictly speaking, "completely impossible."[17] By now, the "drama of non-communication," inaugurated by Ionesco and Beckett, with due acknowledgment to Chekhov, has become almost a standard formula of the *avant-garde* theatre, and has been discussed and analysed at length, in particular by Adamov and Jean Vauthier.[18] Obviously, any principle of total non-communication is necessarily something of a paradox for a dramatist, "for the very fact of writing for the stage and of causing plays to be performed would place me in a position of flagrant contradiction with any such assertion."[19] For Ionesco, the question is not so much one of a total failure to communicate—the one example of a complete breakdown, the deaf-mute orator who provides the *dénouement* to *Les Chaises*, is melodramatic, crude in its symbolism, and drastically unsubtle compared with the rest of the play —as of a radical distortion of thought or purpose under the influence of words. The power of words is such that they seem to promise everything—

OLD WOMAN: It's as we speak that we find our ideas, our words, ourselves, too, in our own words, and the city, the garden, perhaps everything comes back and we're not orphans any more. . . .[20]

—even an escape from solitude; yet in moments of crisis, almost invariably, the promise is left unfulfilled, or else fulfilled in so distorted a manner, that the impression of nightmare is only intensified. In Ionesco's world, the massive impenetrability of language-as-an-object is so great, its tendency to meaninglessness so profound, that the effort required to imbue a word with genuine meaning exhausts all the available energy of the speaker; he has no reserve of mental concentration left within him, either to correlate language and gesture, or to adapt his language specifically to the situation of the listener. And the listener, himself preoccupied with the same problems, therefore rarely listens, or catches only the last word, or the accompanying and ill-correlated gesture, and replies in similar fashion, so that, in spite of the possibility of communication, in fact nothing is achieved—or achieved only on the level of meaninglessness.

Ionesco is a master of this art of *partial* communication. His characters seem to have stepped out of some early Byzantine painting—each turned naïvely full-face to the audience, yet simultaneously sketching ineffective gestures in another direction. *A* speaks; *B* listens; *B* then replies as though *A* had conveyed no information whatsoever:

> MARY: I am the maid. I have just spent a very pleasant afternoon. I went to the pictures with a man and saw a film with some women. When we came out of the cinema we went and drank some brandy and some milk, and afterwards we read the newspaper.
> MRS SMITH: I hope you spent a pleasant afternoon. I hope you went to the pictures with a man and drank some brandy and some milk.
> MR SMITH: And the newspaper![21]

This process reaches its logical conclusion in the unforgettable "dialogues-in-counterpoint" of *Le Tueur* and of *Rhinocéros*, where not one but several conversations are carried on simultaneously in the same vein, each character, absorbed by his own obsessions, picking up the half-heard cues, not of his own, but of someone else's interlocutor. These scenes alone, by their technical virtuosity, would suffice to place Ionesco in the forefront of contemporary dramatists. It is, however, in the field of emotional rather than of rational communication that the lack of correlation between thought, word, and gesture becomes particularly apparent. Emotional responses, far more than intellectual ones, derive from the "inner life," are inseparable from "total reality"; yet, because of the fear which their very irrationality inspires in the conscious mind, these responses have been all the more rigidly systematised by social conventions, exteriorised and thus rendered meaningless. The "socially acceptable" stylisation of emotional responses is one of the main themes of *Jacques ou la soumission* and of its sequel, *L'Avenir est dans les œufs*. Society *requires* certain emotional attitudes to be expressed in certain formulæ, and woe unto him who fails to conform:

JACQUELINE [*to* JACQUES]: Grandfather is dead [*she gives* JACQUES *a violent nudge*].

FATHER-JACQUES: Your grandfather is dead [*she gives him another nudge.* JACQUES *still makes no reaction. . .*].

FATHER-JACQUES: Don't you understand that your grandfather is dead?

JACQUES: No, I don't understand that grandfather is dead.

MOTHER-JACQUES [*whining*]: Poor child. Your reflexes must have stopped working. We must get them going again.

JACQUES *falls into* JACQUELINE'S *arms; she stands him up again. For a few moments his face remains expressionless. The parents, the grandmother, and the sister search for a sign on the young man's face. They appear very worried.*

MOTHER-JACQUES: Cry! Let yourself go, my boy, and cry! [*Silence.*] Come on then! [*Silence. Suddenly* JACQUES *starts to sob.*]

FATHER-JACQUES: There we are, at last! That's done it![22]

In consequence, of course, these formulæ promptly lose whatever meaning they once possessed, and to the intellectual and spiritual solitude of man is added his emotional isolation. Nothing can touch him, least of all pity for others. And if (as Rousseau argues) pity for others is the very cornerstone of ethics, then ethics likewise belongs to the domain of the absurd. This emotional isolation, or rather imperviousness, of the individual in Ionesco's world is nowhere more marked than in his reaction to violent death. Marie, in *La Leçon*, faced with the murder of the Girl-Student; Madeleine, in *Victimes du devoir*, confronted with the death of the Detective at the hands of Nicolas d'Eu ("It's such a pity it had to happen in *our* flat");[23] Amédée, telling the tale of the woman who drowned, reveal one and all an identical attitude of egotistical indifference. This, in the fullest sense of the word, is "alienation":

> AMÉDÉE: Listen. . . . You know I was in the country one day fishing . . . a woman fell into the water and shouted for help. As I can't swim—and anyway the fish were biting—I stayed where I was and left her to drown.[24]

This ineradicable egotism, this total failure of emotional response, necessarily vitiates the whole concept of love and marriage. A surprising amount of Ionesco's drama is concerned, directly or indirectly, with the problems of marriage, and even his lovers (Bérenger and Daisy Bérenger and Dany, Jacques and Roberte II) from the first envisage their relationship in terms of a conventional *ménage*. In the structure of the plays themselves, the theme is usually secondary; but, almost invariably, it forms an important element of the background.

Love belongs to the domain of the irrational; it is a major ingredient of the "inner life," the most immediate and accessible experience of "total reality." So also are the primeval impulses of sex, which—almost alone— offer a kind of mysterious promise of communication expressed through touch, through images, through the wild and "clownish" poetry of *Jacques*:

ROBERTE II: Would you like the Sahara horse, from the city in the sands?

JACQUES: The metropolis of the desert! . . .

ROBERTE II: All in brick, all the houses are in brick, the pavements blaze . . . the flames rave beneath . . . crackling air and red, red dust.

JACQUES: Dusty fire.

ROBERTE II: The inhabitants died long ago, dried-up corpses in their homes.

JACQUES: Behind closed shutters. Behind the gates of red wrought iron.

ROBERTE II: Not a man in the empty streets. Not a beast. Not a bird. Not a blade of grass, however parched. Not a rat, not a fly. . . .[25]

But once again, precisely because "love" is an upsurge from the dark regions of irrationality, the bourgeois mind, the mind obsessed with logic and conformity, has clamped down upon it in terror, has stifled it and pushed it back into the regions whence it came. In a rationalistic social system, love is inadmissible—as More and Campanella and Cabet and Zamyatin knew only too well. In normal circumstances, Ionesco is only marginally concerned with social satire as such, but here his principles of "universalism" desert him. *Jacques* and *L'Avenir*, *Amédée* and *Victimes*, are vicious and grotesquely caricatured portraits of the bourgeois system at work in love and marriage. Marriage without love; marriage as a family convenience, a social function; marriage as a means to reproduction (and the woman weighed as so many stone and pounds of potentially fertile flesh); marriage as the murderer of love (the corpse in *Amédée*), even where love existed in the first place; marriage as the shield to preserve society from the intolerable awareness of sex—this is the penalty society has to pay for worshipping its own comfort. In this deliberate destruction and betrayal of the inner life, for fear "of what the

E

neighbours say," woman, in Ionesco's world, is guiltier by far than man. Adam is betrayed by Eve. Choubert is betrayed by Madeleine (*Victimes du devoir*), and betrayed in the most cruel and sordid manner, to the police; Bérenger (*Rhinocéros*) is betrayed by Daisy, just as the earlier Bérenger (*Le Tueur*) is betrayed by a glossy and indifferent Dany. But it is in *Amédée* that the fear, the egotism, the stupidity and the emotional barrenness of woman is brought out in all its sordid splendour. In this gruesome portrait of marital bickering, loneliness, and frustration—a portrait whose inspiration is fully worthy of Strindberg's *Dance of Death*—it is Madeleine who is for ever embittering the quarrels, dragging Amédée with her ever further downwards into her morass of despair and solitude and bourgeois misery. Much of the latter part of *Amédée*, including the symbolic "dream-scene" in Act II, is technically clumsy and contrived; yet the play as a whole is a moving and convincing study of a marriage without communication—a marriage where, in the absence of real contact, whether through love or sex, the only substitute is words; and words themselves can only offer an illusion of communication when they are violent, bitter, and unforgivable. In the absence of love, Amédée and Madeleine *must* quarrel: it is the only semblance of communication they possess. Amédée has perhaps an inkling of the truth; but Madeleine is cold and blind and *womanish*:

AMÉDÉE: Poor Madeleine! What a terrible time you've had. Do you know, Madeleine, if we loved each other, if we really loved each other, none of this would be important. Why don't we try to love each other, *please*, Madeleine? Love puts everything right, you know, it changes life. Do you believe me, can you understand?

MADELEINE: Oh! Leave me alone!

AMÉDÉE: I know it does!.... Love makes up for everything.

MADELEINE: Don't talk rubbish! I can't see love getting rid of this dead body. Nor hate either, for that matter. It's got nothing to do with feelings.[26]

If love seems to offer an escape from solitude upward, in the direction of a super-rational communication, sex offers the same thing downward, via the confusion and the chaos of animal experience. In a world where rational communication has failed, eroticism has a primary function to perform—a function which may, of its very nature, be grotesque (*Les Chaises, Le Tableau*) or fantastic (*Le Salon de l'automobile*), but which is none the less an essential constituent of total reality. Rationally to repress the erotic impulse is to court disaster; for unfailingly it will break out again in some more violent form—the psychopathic mania of the Professor in *La Leçon*, the horrifying sadistic glee of Madeleine as she watches her husband tortured (*Victimes du devoir*). There is a certain element of Freudianism in Ionesco, which comes nearest to the surface in *Victimes du devoir*; the emphasis, however, is far from that of Freud, closer to that of Georges Bataille.[27] The sexual subconscious—indeed, *all* the subconscious—is not an explanation of conscious awareness and behaviour; it is a substitute for consciousness when the latter, through its very narrowness, has failed to fulfil its promise. Love, sex, dream, poetry, nightmare—these are the only means of communication which subsist in a world where rationality has finally strangled the sense of language.

REFERENCES

1. N.R.F., I. 52–3 (I. 118–19).
2. Jean Vannier, "Langages de l'avant-garde," p. 32.
3. "La Tragédie du langage . . . ," p. 3.
4. *Op. cit.*, p. 4.
5. *Op. cit.*, p. 5.
6. *Ibid.*

7. N.R.F., ii. 251–2 (iii.154–5).

8. N.R.F., i. 94, 96, 99 (i. 122, 124, 127).

9. N.R.F., i. 49 (i. 115: the Watson translation here does not convey an equivalent).

10. Vannier, "Langages de l'avant-garde," p. 33.

11. "Point de départ," pp. 17–18.

12. *Rhinocéros*, pp. 196–7 (*Plays*, iv. 106).

13. N.R.F., i. 78 (i. 25).

14. N.R.F., i. 121–2 (i. 149–50).

15. N.R.F., i. 39–40 (i. 106).

16. L.S., pp. 157–8.

17. "Ionesco à l'heure anglaise," in *Théâtre populaire*, No. 34, p. 133.

18. Cp. esp. Adamov, "Note préliminaire," in *Théâtre*, ii. 8–9.

19. "Ionesco à l'heure anglaise," p. 133.

20. N.R.F., i. 134 (i. 47).

21. N.R.F., i. 23 (i. 91).

22. N.R.F., ii. 215–16 (iv. 127).

23. N.R.F., i. 227 (ii. 315).

24. N.R.F., i. 268 (ii. 189–90).

25. N.R.F., i. 118 (i. 146).

26. N.R.F., i. 282 (ii. 202–3).

27. Cp. Georges Bataille, *L'Erotisme*, Paris 1958.

CHAPTER IV

THE VOID AT THE CENTRE OF THINGS

If Ionesco's analysis of the destiny of man stopped short at man-in-society, the situation might still be tolerable. But, having once embarked upon his vertiginous conflict with the absurd, there is no drawing-back. The isolation of man through the breakdown of language, disastrous as it is, is not in itself the determining factor of existence; man is already isolated by the very conditions of his being, and the failure of words is merely symptomatic of a far profounder solitude. At the level of social or political discussion, Ionesco always tends to contrast the inner life of the individual with the superficial and exterior reality of "man absorbed in his social context", thus suggesting or implying that the total reality of the subconscious is capable of providing him with something of that stability and identity which rational "society" denies him. But not all Ionesco's characters are at grips with society all the time; every now and then there comes an instant of lucidity, of self-discovery, when they try to speak to us of their real existence. And these are the moments when the terror of absurdity reaches its highest pitch of intensity; for only then do we realise that, between the total and the sham reality, there is, in the last analysis, no effective contrast. Both are gratuitous, both are void, both are meaningless; the choice is never wholly between true and false, real and unreal, but merely between an intolerable recognition of the absurd, and an equally intolerable refusal to admit it.

"There was a kind of chaotic vacuum inside me," says

Bérenger in *Le Tueur*, describing the innermost experience of his soul,

> I was overcome with the immense sadness you feel at the moment of tragic and intolerable separation. The old gossips came out of their courtyards and split my eardrums with their screeching voices, the dogs barked, and I felt lost among all those people, all those *things*. . . .[1]

This is one of the key passages in the understanding of Ionesco's cosmogony, for it reveals the final significance of that cacophonous barrage of discords and platitudes of which so much of his work consists. Words petrified into objects, dense masses of unco-ordinated meaninglessness coagulated into a sort of menacing *musique concrète*—these in themselves would not be intolerable, were it not for the void, the "chaotic vacuum" within, which these lifeless but proliferating fossils fill instantaneously to the brim, so that the inner life, as well as the outer, is usurped and victimised by *things*. The word-made-object usurps the inner as well as the outer man, because the inner life has nothing to oppose to the usurpation, save only two contrasting "states of being."

In the opening scene of *Tueur sans gages*, Bérenger portrays in highly dramatic terms the tension between these two conflicting "poles of awareness," and thereby comes closer than any other character, perhaps, to uttering Ionesco's own thoughts. Stripped of their breathless tone and imagery, Bérenger's experiences correspond point for point with those of the dramatist himself, as he has described them in "Point de départ":

> Two fundamental states of consciousness are at the root of all my plays. Sometimes one dominates, sometimes the other; sometimes they are mingled. These two basic feelings are those of evanescence on the one hand and of heaviness on the other; of emptiness and

of an overabundance of presence; of the unreal transparency of the world, and of its opaqueness; of light and of heavy shadow.[2]

Neither of these awarenesses, however, provides a means of dominating or controlling the outside world. Both are passive, both are involuntary, subjective *reactions to* the fact of existence in a material universe; both are at bottom a degree of consciousness of the absurd. The lighter of the two sensations leads directly to an overpowering and obsessive *angoisse*:

We seem to see through everything in a universe without space, made up only of light and colour; all our existence, all the history of the world becomes at this moment useless, senseless, impossible. . . .[3]

A stage further in this experience, and "anguish is suddenly transformed into liberty"; but this total liberty offers no escape from the absurd, it is merely an awareness still more intensified. There is a "wonder of being," a "new and surprising consciousness of our existence"; but it is still a consciousness of existence in a

world that appears illusory and fictitious, where human behaviour reveals its absurdity, and all history its absolute uselessness; all reality, all language seems to become disjointed, to fall apart, to empty itself of meaning, so that, since all is devoid of importance, what else can one do but laugh at it?[4]

Thus the ultimate *angoisse* of Ionesco's own experience is at the same time the source and mainspring of his awareness of the comic; on the other hand (and this is proof, if any is needed, that the two states of consciousness are interrelated, inseparable), much of the actual material of comedy is derived from the opposite pole of perception, the awareness of a world in which

matter fills everything, takes up all space, annihilates all liberty under its weight; the horizon shrinks and the

world becomes a stifling dungeon. Speech crumbles,
but in another way [. . .]. Words, obviously devoid of
magic, are replaced by accessories, by objects. . . .[5]

This totally irrational basis of perception begins notice-
ably to permeate Ionesco's characters with the creation of
Choubert in *Victimes du devoir*. Choubert, who is "heavy
when he ought to be light, too light when he ought to be
heavy, unbalanced, has no grip on reality,"[6] discovers in
himself, at the crisis of his senseless search for "Mallot
with a *t*," a tendency to levitate—a spiritual potentiality
which is in fact realised by Amédée as he sails away
among the fireworks and the constellations. The alternative to matter, in fact, is emptiness; and man, released
from the meaninglessness of objects, is totally free—to
merge with the meaninglessness of space! Whether, in
fact, both poles of awareness are *equally* meaningless is,
however, the central problem of Ionesco's drama. To the
Bérenger of *Le Tueur*, the evanescent state is revealed
with an intensity which seems to promise, as it were, a
new dimension of significance, a dimension which is
illusory, but not necessarily unreal; and even his final
annihilation does not invalidate this promise, since it is
precisely the rational rather than the irrational Bérenger
who is annihilated. The later Bérenger of *Rhinocéros*, on
the other hand, discovers his own significant indivi-
duality through a diametrically-opposite experience,
while in this case, it is the doomed rationalist Jean, the
Cornelian apostle of will-power and duty, who feels the
touch of evanescence:

BÉRENGER: I'm conscious of my body all the time, as
    if it were made of lead, or as if I were carrying an-
    other man around on my back. I can't seem to get
    used to myself. I don't even know if I *am* me. Then
    as soon as I take a drink, the lead slips away, and I
    recognize myself, I become me again.

JEAN: That's just being fanciful. Look at me, Bérenger,
I weigh more than you do. And yet I feel light, light
as a feather [*He flaps his arms as if about to fly*]. . . .[7]

The conclusion of the argument (if one can use the
term, when the subject-matter is so elusive, so over-
shadowed by the darkness that engulfs the outer regions
of experience) is that both states, lucidly apprehended,
deliberately explored, may enable the individual to *define
himself* in a way not possible in rational analysis—in other
words, that the lucid perception of meaninglessness is in
itself a meaningful—the only meaningful—act.

What is clear, however, is that the achievement of self-
awareness, or self-definition, through the awareness of
materiality is, to the average human being, intolerable
(as indeed it is to Roquentin). Bérenger deadens the
angoisse of his perception with drink; and it is significant
that another of Ionesco's voices from the inner world, the
anonymous toff in top hat and tails who, in *Le Tueur*,
alone dares to stand in opposition to La Mère Pipe, is
similarly a drunkard. By contrast, the perception of
"evanescence," the vision of a transparent world of
light and incandescence, is, or can be, a poetic experience of the highest order, bordering on the realms of
mysticism.

The insistent recurrence of this dream of luminosity
and incandescence alone is evidence of its obsessive
quality; nor does it confine itself to the text of the play,
but overflows into the stage-directions, where the problem of lighting outweighs all other technical considerations.[8] The opening of *Tueur sans gages* is a completely
wordless drama of light, a conflict of "November-grey"
and "blue and white" illumination constituting "the sole
elements of the *décor*"; likewise in the ballet, *Apprendre à
marcher*, the stage is transformed gradually into "a
luminous garden" (Scene 3), while later "a staircase
appears in the background, infinite and brightly lumi-

nous" (Scene 4). In these stage-directions, the chief
constituents of the dream are already apparent: light,
usually without heat (but not always without pain), often
with a bluish quality; sometimes statically incarnated in
the transparency of a formal garden, sometimes in violent
motion, sweeping upwards and shedding cascades of
coloured sparks as it mounts. That the vision was, in
origin at least, subconscious, seems to be proved by its
almost incongruous appearance amid the parody and
platitudes of *La Cantatrice*, breaking out in Mary's
"poem":

> ... Women on fire
> Eyes on fire
> The blood caught fire
> The sand caught fire
> The birds caught fire
> The fish caught fire
> The moon caught fire
> The ashes caught fire
> The smoke caught fire
> The fire caught fire
> Caught fire, caught fire, caught
> fire ... caught fire. ... [9]

—and in the Fireman's characteristic rejoinder:

> It's so true. It's so exactly the way I think myself, just
> my own idea of life, my ideal way of life. [10]

Even the decrepit ancients of *Les Chaises* are haunted by
the memory of a garden with a luminous city beyond, and
so searing is the memory that their very speech disintegrates into a kind of paralytic rhymed doggerel. [11] On
the other hand, Jacques's vision of the burning stallion
with its fiery mane and wings of flame, with "flames
shooting from his nostrils and his ears," [12] galloping
through the dead-lands of the desert, has a high poetic
quality rivalled only by the greatest of the Surrealists;

and even when love has withered, killed by the soulless social routine of domesticity and reproduction, the dream of "a fountain of light, incandescent water, fire of ice, snows of fire,"[13] still has the power to strike a spark from poor Jacques's dying imagination.

But these early versions of the vision are no more than preliminary sketches for its full development in Choubert, Amédée and Bérenger. Jacques, for a while at least, could share his dream with Roberte II; but characteristically, Choubert and Amédée, who are more absorbed in this inner light, more deeply dependent on it, meet with nothing but contempt and hostility from their womenfolk. "And I bet you he thinks he's a poet! A lot of bad Parnassian-Symbolic-Surrealism," is Madeleine's bitter retort to Choubert's "magic garden . . . and flowers of fire in the night";[14] while the second Madeleine pours even colder waters of common sense over Amédée's ecstatic exaltation:

AMÉDÉE: Look, Madeleine . . . all the acacia trees are aglow. Their blossoms are bursting open and shooting up to the sky. The full-blown moon is flooding the Heavens with light, a *living* planet. The Milky Way is like creamy fire. Honeycombs, countless galaxies, comets' tails, celestial ribbons, rivers of molten silver, and brooks, lakes and oceans of palpable light [. . .]. Sheaves of blossoming snow, trees in the sky, gardens and meadows . . . domes and cupolas . . . columns and temples [. . .]. And space, space, infinite space!

MADELEINE: Don't waste time. What's the matter with you? The night air's coming in. We shall both catch cold.[15]

Decidedly, woman has no place within the "radiant city." Her dream, if she has one, if she can escape the dreary confinement of reality and routine, is of water rather than of fire—Freudian echoes, perhaps, of a sexual subconscious, but derived at the same time from the waters of Styx, of oblivion. It is the "waters of solitude" which surround the weird mansion of *Les Chaises*, and which promise extinction to its ancient guardians; while both Roberte II and Choubert's Madeleine hark back distinctly to this world of marshland and humidity. "Come ... don't be afraid," says Roberte II,

> I'm all moist. ... I've a necklace of ooze, my breasts are melting, my pelvis is soft, I've water in my crevices [. . .]. In my womb there are ponds and swamps. ... I've a house of clay, where I always feel cool [. . .]. You plunge deep and dissolve ... in the rain of my streaming hair. My mouth is flowing, streaming my legs, streaming my shoulders bare, my hair is flowing, everything flows and streams, the sky's a stream, the stars strow and fleam. . . .[16]

The contrast here is too sharp to be accidental. Ionesco's mistrust of women has roots that go extremely deep. The Architect, for all his impersonality, his tincture of officialdom, none the less listens sympathetically to Bérenger's intimations of immortality, his memory of a world where "the light grew more and more brilliant and still lost none of its softness, it had become so dense you could almost breathe it, it had become the air itself, you could drink it like clear water," where "it was as if there were four suns in the sky";[17] yet Dany, the beautiful blond Dany, not merely turns a very deaf ear to Bérenger's exhortations, but can think of nothing but *escape* from the miraculous Garden City with "its sunny streets and avenues bathed in light."[18]

Obviously, then, the absurdity of evanescence has implications which are in themselves not necessarily meaningless, at least within the limited context of human experience. As a source of exaltation, of art and poetry, it has already a *raison d'être*; for art alone of all material phenomena, in Ionesco's philosophy, is self-justifying, is sufficient reason unto itself, is perhaps even a revelation of something beyond itself, just as a cathedral "may reveal to us the laws of architecture, and perhaps even those of the construction of the universe—laws which are probably reflected in our own mind, since our mind is able to discover them within itself."[19] The absurdity of evanescence is the root of art; and art, as both *L'Impromptu* and *Le Tueur* insist, is the "projection upon the stage of the world within."[20] *Le Tueur*, on the other hand, almost suggests that the dream is realisable—literally realisable in terms of bricks and mortar, main drainage and electric light. Not that the "radiant city" is the ultimate solution; but at least it is an improvement upon the back-to-back townships, the slums and the sorry tenements of industrial Europe. "You know," says Bérenger,

> I do so need another life, a new life. Different surroundings, a different setting [. . .]. A setting, *that's* just superficial, an artistic consideration, unless it's, how shall I say, a setting, a background that would answer some profound need inside, which would be somehow [. . .] the projection, the continuation of the universe inside you. Only, to project this universe within, some outside help is needed: some kind of material, physical light, a world that is objectively new. Gardens, blue sky, or the spring, which corresponds to the universe inside and offers a chance of recognition, which is like a translation or an anticipation of that universe, or a mirror in which its own smile could be reflected. . . .[21]

In one brief passage, Ionesco goes even further, and suggests that the very ubiquity, the very omnipotence, of the absurd contains its own denial, and that "maybe there is a reason, over and above *our* reason, for existing. Everything is so absurd, that even *that* is possible."[22] But this is uncharacteristic: not because it is logically contradictory (Ionesco has always—and quite fairly—maintained his right to contradict himself), but because it conflicts with the profound and ineradicable pessimism which pervades his work no less than that of Beckett. For, over and above the absurdity of life, there hovers the absurdity of death. And where death is, there can be no optimism. What act or thought or man is *not* meaningless, when the end of all is annihilation? The "radiant city', may be an improvement on the slums of Roubaix or Manchester; but what is the most splendid of garden suburbs in the context of final obliteration? The fact of death, and no less than this, the fear of death, is the one experience, the one emotion common to all humanity; it dominates the subconscious, it is the ultimate *community* of man. "I find it distinctly *vexing*, being mortal," Ionesco is once reported to have said; and in the same vein he declared to Georges Lerminier: "An optimistic drama is a downright impossibility."[23]

Death is the one constant theme which gives unity to Ionesco's theatre; sooner or later, the cadaveric quality of words is transmitted to the living organism, and there are few among his major plays with neither corpse nor killer. So obsessive, indeed, is this preoccupation—as a student, he once embarked on a thesis entitled Themes of Sin and Death in French Literature since Baudelaire— that it becomes important to determine its exact role in Ionesco's philosophy. On the one hand, one is tempted to see it as an *a posteriori* rationalisation, arrived at by the conscious mind in order to explain and to relate the fears and anguishes which derive from a subconscious perception of absurdity, much as Lupasco's purely technical-scientific argument against Aristotelian logic is called into service to justify an intuitive awareness of the failure of nineteenth-century materialism. On the other hand, as Father Joseph and his Calvarian nuns discovered, the actual contemplation of death can lead to a state of mystic exaltation not dissimilar from that experienced by Choubert and by Bérenger; dwell for long enough upon the ultimate absurdity, upon the final triumph of inanimate over animate existence, and there may ensue that trance-like state of dissociation from material reality, well known among the mystics of the East.

The fact that Ionesco, in one passage at least, associates the death-theme with a childhood experience inclines one at first to give precedence to the second interpretation. Recalling a walk with his mother one winter evening through the grey and crowded Place de Vaugirard, the thought which haunts him is that, of all the nameless figures who filled this scrap of street-scene salvaged from a vanished childhood, not one, in all probability, still exists:

> Whenever the picture of this street lives again in my memory, and when I consider that today almost all those people are dead, everything strikes me indeed as shadow and evanescence. I am seized with dizziness, with anguish. There, in effect, goes the world: a desert of dying shadows.[24]

For all its vividness, however, this is not, in itself, a childhood impression; it is an adult's commentary upon a memory of childhood, and it is, moreover, directly associated with another early memory (legacy of a later adolescence in Fascist-inclined Roumania) of brutality, of "futile and sordid bursts of fury, of sudden screams stifled by silence, of shadows swallowed up for ever in the night."[25] The uncharacteristically melodramatic tone of this last quotation suggests a rationalisation, as does also the intellectual twist or conceit which transforms the elemental fear of death into a prick of wounded vanity: "I am afraid of death, certainly; but I am besides deeply wounded in my self-esteem."[26] This interpretation is perhaps borne out by the slightly strained symbolism of the various death-figures or images in the plays: the Corpse in *Amédée*; the double suicide of *Les Chaises*; Edouard, with his graveyard cough and his funereal costume, in *Le Tueur*—and of course, the Killer himself.

Be this as it may, however, the contemplation of death occupies an essential position in Ionesco's thought. As a critic, he sums up Shakespeare's *Richard II* as "an illustration of that truth of which we do not think, and which is simple and infinitely banal: *I die, you die, he dies* . . .";[27] to which conclusion, both Bérenger and Edouard provide the echo: "What's the good of it all, what's the good, if it's only to bring us to this [. . .].[28] We are all going to die. That's the only *alienation* that counts!"[29] The terror, however, resides, not so much in the fact of death itself, as in its inherent senselessness. Not only does it destroy the meaningfulness of all that goes before it; it is itself devoid of meaning. The concept of achieving something by death is totally alien to Ionesco; the word "sacrifice" is absent from his vocabulary—like "hope," it is "not a French word any more, or Turkish, or Polish . . . Belgian perhaps . . . and even then. . . ."[30] In Lerminier's telling phrase, "Ionesco's Corpses are *gratuitous*; they solve nothing."[31] But there is worse: for not only is man condemned inevitably to a natural extinction in absurdity, but seems, even while alive, to be doing his utmost to hasten the arrival of death. Ionesco is among those whose universe—what part of it remained intact after the Nazification of Roumania and the German occupation of France—was finally shattered by Hiroshima. His awareness of death is heightened by an awareness of the impending horror of life. "If we all thought about all the misfortunes of mankind," observes the Architect in *Le Tueur*, "we could never go on living. And we *must* live!"[32] And Ionesco himself, when taken to task by a student-interviewer over the paradoxical nature of his assertion, "Reality, *unlike dreams*, can turn into a nightmare",[33] retorted:

I really have the feeling that life is nightmarish, that it is painful, unendurable as a bad dream. Just glance around you: wars, catastrophes and disasters, hatreds

and persecutions, death awaiting us on every side
[. . .]. We are made to be immortal, and yet we die.
It's horrible, it can't be taken seriously.[34]

This pessimism provides a sort of continuous ground-
bass to Ionesco's drama: "Everything, as I see it, is an
aberration."[35] Even the climate seems to conspire against
the possibility of human happiness, whether it be the
"dirty snow and bitter winds"[36] of Bérenger's experience,
or the "everlasting winter" that dogged the life of
Choubert's Job-like father.[37] Here and there, even
Ionesco himself seems slightly embarrassed by the extent
of his own pessimism: he refers self-consciously to his
"bad temper,"[38] or tries to soften the impact of it by some
more "positive," yet curiously unconvincing assertion:
"If I denounce the absurd, I transcend the absurd by the
very fact of my denunciation. For by what right should I
declare a thing to be absurd, unless I had before me the
image—whether sharply or vaguely defined, no matter—
of something that was *not* absurd?"[39] Yet, paradoxically,
the very intensity of Ionesco's pessimism is in itself, not a
numbing, but a vivifying experience. Bérenger is hyper-
sensitive to the reality of life; of him, as of the hero of
Robert Graves' *Lost Love*, it might be said,

> His eyes are quickened so with grief,
> He can watch a grass or leaf
> Every instant grow. . . .

His awareness of the void at the centre of things gives him
an acute sense of being apart from the common run of
humanity; not a Romantic "aristocrat of misfortune,"
but simply a *misfit* in the routine machinations of destiny.
"I'm not made for the work I'm doing," he protests, "I
can't get used to it. I just can't get *used* to life";[40] and
Amédée suffers from a similar spiritual inferiority-
complex:

Anyone else could manage better than I do. I'm like

F

a helpless child, I'm defenceless. I'm a misfit . . . I
wasn't made to live in the twentieth century. . . .[41]

In Amédée, this embryonic quality of awareness is
eventually swamped in wave after wave of failure, weakness, and self-pity; but Bérenger, despite all his shortcomings, is made of spiritually sterner stuff. He is an
Outsider, an *homme révolté*, a metaphysical insurgent,
rebelling first and foremost against the very absurdity of
existence, but still more against the stupidity of those who
fail to recognise it for what it is. In Bérenger, the characteristic of constant surprise, which, in *La Cantatrice*, was
merely a reflex reaction to an anti-logical universe, takes
on a profounder significance. The death of Dany brings
home to him the fact that existence is not merely absurd
but intolerable, and therefore *cannot* be accepted:

We can't, we mustn't let things go on like this! It's
got to stop! It's got to stop! [. . .] It can't go on! We
must *do* something! We must, we must, we must![42]

But what overwhelms him beyond belief is not so much
the terror and the fear of death, as the calm and stolic
acceptance of it by the ordinary run of mortals. If death
is the central theme of Ionesco's drama, the stupidity and
self-deception of mankind faced with death is a necessary
corollary. No writer since Flaubert has been so mesmerised, so utterly fascinated, by the impenetrable *bêtise*
of the average man. From *La Cantatrice* to *Scène à quatre*
every conceivable degree of thick-headedness is lovingly
and caressingly analysed and lingered over. Nor is there
any hope of cure: stupidity and self-deception are the
very heritage of man, ingrained, ineradicable; humanity
is born dumb, blinkered, and doomed. And yet, in its
very stupidity, lies its salvation; for how could it live
were it aware of the truth? How could it exist beneath the
threat of the hydrogen bomb, unless it contrived to forget
about it, and, like the builders of Kafka's *Tower of Babel*,

so clutter up the horizon with irrelevancies, disputes and insignificant arguments, that the ultimate reality was lost sight of altogether? "Do you know," demands Bérenger,

do you know the things that happen in the world, awful things, in our town, terrible things, you can't imagine... quite near here... comparatively close... morally speaking it's actually *here*![44]

And it is essentially the same Bérenger who, in *Rhinocéros*, utters that last despairing *cri de cœur* at the sight of the placid, cow-like docility of man, faced with a situation which is, both physically and metaphysically, intolerable:

I'm frankly surprised. I'm very, *very* surprised. I can't get over it.[45]

Destiny has placed man in an impossible situation, and his natural reaction is to shut his eyes and to bury his head in the sand. To the average mortal, the merest glimpse of the absurd is disconcerting, if not terrifying; and he has reason to be afraid, for the first glimpse of the absurd is the first moment of lucidity, and thenceforward there is no turning back: lucidity breeds further awareness, further awareness breeds more lucidity, until, in the end he is faced, like Bérenger, with two intolerable alternatives: to accept the absurd, or to revolt against it— knowing full well that it is the condition of existence, and therefore that revolt is again absurdity, raised to the nth degree. This is the *angoisse* of Ionesco's world. Man is not at one with his surroundings, the context in which he exists; "the universe itself provides the obstacle,"[46] and he is at odds with it. And the symbol of this conflict is, on the one hand, the subconscious fears, the "forms of anguish difficult to define,"[47] the "nameless regrets, the aimless remorse,"[48] the "mysterious nostalgias,"[49] which form the common heritage of man; and on the other, the triumphant proliferation of the senseless world of things. This anguish, precisely because it is subconscious, is not always immediately apparent; more often it is betrayed by a kind of surrender, a dull refusal to accept the promise of life, the failure (as in *Le Nouveau Locataire*) of the last attempt to defend the void within against the encroachment of material objects. Bérenger, on the other hand, feels "out of place in life, among people";[50] for him, the anguish of the subconscious has begun to acquire an outline—blurred, but none the less impressive—in the conscious mind: "Solitude seems to oppress me. And so does the company of other people [. . .]. Life is an abnormal business [. . .]. I sometimes wonder if I exist myself."[51]

Awareness such as this, however, is the exception rather than the rule. The majority of Ionesco's characters are too stupid, too heavily-protected by their armour of social attitudes, to understand or voice their own *angoisse*; and so it is not they themselves, but their surroundings, that offer visible evidence of their plight. Bérenger declares war on the rhinoceroses: but it is the chairs, the furniture, the coffee-cups, the corpses of men, of systems and of words, which declare war on Jacques and Amédée, on the Caretakers and the New Tenant, on the Martins and the Smiths. "I have tried," asserts Ionesco

> to exteriorise the anguish of my characters through objects, to endow the scenery with speech, to give a visual quality to the dramatic action, to render concrete images of terror or regret, of remorse or alienation. . . .[52]

The essential quality, however, of this anguish is its universality. It is the common bond of all humanity, independent of time or place or social condition. When Ionesco defines himself as a "classic dramatist," it is this that lies in the forefront of his mind: to rediscover the *universality* of Racinian drama as opposed to the "historical" and "local" and "social" dramas which triumph in the theatre from the days of Diderot and Nivelle de la Chaussée. To transcend the narrow bounds of the political community, to re-establish a universal bond common without exception to all mankind—such is Ionesco's ambition. This theme recurs at nearly every level of Ionesco's theoretical writing, from his verdict on Molière to his criticism of Sartre and Brecht and Kenneth Tynan:

> What is important is to discover what there is in common between myself and, say, a shoemaker in the eighteenth century; and I believe that he and I are basically alike. I believe that men in every century have been afraid of death, just as I am afraid of death; and it is to this fundamental identity that I have tried to cling. And that is why I rather disapprove of stressing individual differences when one is creating a "character." What interests me above all is the deep-rooted identity of people, precisely because my need is to establish contact with all men everywhere.[53]

Thus the theme of death, the final symbol of absurdity, not merely determines the content, but also, to a considerable degree, dictates the form, of Ionesco's drama. If his characters are deliberately blurred in outline, if they are shifting and interchangeable, this is due, not only to the disintegration of rational psychology under the impact of the absurd, but also to the fact that their "humanity" is defined in terms of subconscious rather than conscious criteria. And at the root of the subconscious lies the "true community" of *fear*. Politically, socially, all the world may lie between the Yogi and the Commissar; yet each in his irrational dreams, his undefined nostalgias, his subconscious uncertainties, is united with the other. The conscious awareness may set up countless rational defences against the menace of annihilation; but at bottom, "we are one and all afraid of death. Deeper than that there is nothing."[54] If the decade which has just ended has been rightly termed "the Frightened Fifties," then Ionesco is its dramatist *par excellence*.

REFERENCES

1. N.R.F., II. 79 (III. 24–5).
2. "Point de départ," p. 17.
3. Ibid.
4. Op. cit., p. 18.
5. Ibid.
6. N.R.F., I. 215 (II. 304).
7. Rhinocéros, p. 37 (Plays, IV, 18).
8. The influence of Jean Vilar is here probably considerable.
9. N.R.F., I. 48 (I. 114).
10. Ibid.
11. N.R.F., I. 134 (I. 46: Watson's translation here conveys the effect admirably).
12. N.R.F., I. 119 (I. 147).
13. N.R.F., II. 230 (IV. 141).
14. N.R.F., II. 203–4 (II. 293).
15. N.R.F., I. 289–90 (II. 209–210).
16. N.R.F., I. 120 (I. 148).
17. N.R.F., II. 77 (III. 22–3).
18. N.R.F., II. 65 (III. 11).
19. "E.I.o.f.," pp. 188–90.
20. N.R.F., II. 57 (III. 150).
21. N.R.F., II. 73 (III. 18–19).
22. "Celui qui ose ne pas haïr . . . ," pp. 1–2.
23. Georges Lerminier, "Dialogue avec Ionesco," p. 53.
24. "Qu'est-ce que l'avant-garde en 1958?," p. 1.
25. Ibid.
26. Lerminier, "Dialogue avec Ionesco," p. 52.
27. "D. Th.," pp. 14–15.
28. N.R.F., II. 89 (III. 34).
29. N.R.F., II. 145 (III. 83).
30. N.R.F., II. 65 (III. 11).
31. Georges Lerminier, "Clés pour Ionesco," p. 4.
32. N.R.F., II. 91 (III. 36).
33. N.R.F., II. 60 (III. 26).
34. "Entretien," p. 12.
35. Quoted by P. Sarisson in Aux Ecoutes, 16 Jan. 1959.
36. N.R.F., II. 74 (III. 19).
37. N.R.F., I. 197 (II. 287).
38. "Entretien," p. 13.
39. Lerminier, "Dialogue avec Ionesco," p. 52.
40. Rhinocéros, pp. 18–19 (Plays, IV. 7).
41. N.R.F., I. 260 (II. 181).
42. N.R.F., II. 97–8 (III. 42).
43. "Dans les armes de la ville," pp. 3–5. Cp. Fontenelle; "Partout où il y a des hommes, il y a des sottises, et les mêmes sottises" (Dialogues des morts).
44. N.R.F., II. 119 (III. 60).
45. Rhinocéros, p. 150 (Plays, IV. 79).
46. "Finalement," p. 1.
47. Rhinocéros, p. 36 (Plays, IV. 17).
48. "L'Invraisemblable," p. 1.
49. "Ionesco à l'heure anglaise," pp. 133–4.
50. Rhinocéros, p. 36 (Plays, IV. 17).
51. Rhinocéros, p. 39 (Plays, IV. 19).
52. "Le Cœur n'est pas sur la main," pp. 264–5.
53. Reported by Robert Kanters, "Entretien avec Ionesco," in Express, 28 Jan. 1960, p. 37.
54. Lerminier, "Dialogue avec Ionesco," p. 53.

CHAPTER V

UTOPIA AND AFTER

In France, it is enough—almost—that a writer should be profoundly and influentially revolutionary in *form* for the critics to consider him "committed," and committed, without question, to the Left. To belong to the *avant-garde* is *ipso facto* to be against the Establishment; exceptions are so rare—Claudel alone, perhaps, since the beginning of the present century—that even open hostility towards other Left-committed writers counts scarcely in the balance. "Saint Ionesco, the Anti-Brecht," whatever his past history, is still assumed by the majority of French critics to be *un homme de gauche*.

In England, the position is vastly different, for the Great Divide of mutual contempt between politicians and writers has for so long prevailed, while genuinely "committed" men of letters are so much the exception rather than the rule, that English critics are perhaps not wrong to apply the dictum of Paul Guth and to proclaim that "to opt out of politics is to side with the Establishment."[1] It follows, therefore, that Ionesco's doctrine of "belligerent non-commitment" has been subject to widely varying interpretations on different sides of the Channel. In particular, Kenneth Tynan, strongly backed by Orson Welles, has accused Ionesco of trying to "opt out" of politics, and thus has seriously misinterpreted, or at least oversimplified, this important aspect of his work.

For Ionesco's position with regard to politics, like most of his thought, is decidedly complex. Death and the fear of death—the subconscious and the metaphysical—comprise the central themes of his drama, whereas problems of political and social organisation, concerning as they do almost exclusively the conscious and material aspects of existence, can rarely be of more than marginal significance, and in fact may dangerously obscure the real issues at stake. On the other hand, the "horror" of existence and the universal imminence of death, above all the universal awareness of the *fear* of death, are specifically linked with certain definite political combinations in the modern world, and, consequently, these combinations are never negligible. To put the same conclusion in another form: if it is true that Ionesco has roundly condemned both Sartre and Brecht and all "committed" literature, it is no less true that he could never have written the plays by which he is known, if indeed he had written at all, were it not for Hitler and Hiroshima. English criticism, not a little puzzled by the appearance of a major French writer who flatly refuses to harness his theatre to this party or to that, has tended to overlook (because it is concealed) the violence of his onslaught against certain all-too-current political attitudes of our time. But, over and beyond this, there is in addition the fact that to reject the traditional attitudes towards the human condition is *ipso facto* to criticise the current ideologies which these attitudes have bred. A new view of man is in itself an argument for the Left. The heavy-handed sociological tirades of a Wesker may be missing; yet for all that, Ionesco's drama is none the less a drama of dissent. By no argument in the world can a writer who publishes, for preference, in the quasi-anarchist *Cahiers de 'Pataphysique*, or in the off-beat, anti-clerical *Bizarre*; be counted among the pillars of the Establishment.

One fact is incontrovertible: Ionesco is inextricably involved in his own plays, "committed" willy-nilly to the struggles and destiny (if not to the actual language) of his characters. And these characters, despite the dream-surroundings in which they exist, are involved in reality. There is all the difference in the world between imagination and "illusion"; imagination is a means, not of avoiding, but of coming to grips with reality, whereas the philosophy which "deems this world of ours naught but illusion" is not so much wrong, according to Ionesco, as irrelevant. "Right or wrong, no matter; it *seems* real to us, and obviously this reality (however precarious it may prove) is the one we have to deal with."[2] Again and again, Ionesco insists upon the extent of his own intimate participation in the theatre which he has created. "Each play of mine has its roots in a kind of self-analysis," he declares;[3] and elsewhere: "More often than not, the theatre—my theatre—is a confession; all I do is to make personal avowals (incomprehensible, of course, when the listener is deaf—how should it be otherwise?); for what else could I do?"[4] The very intensity of this subjectivism, moreover, carries it above the level of the merely personal, the idiosyncratic. Between the "I" and the "not-I" there is no inherent conflict. The inner world (the "subjective" element) is simply a reflexion of the outer world of "objective" reality; the microcosm, all "tattered and disjointed" as it is, is nothing but the perfect miniature of the macrocosm, "the very mirror and symbol of contradictions on a universal scale."[5] Between "subjective" and "objective" there is no clear line of demarcation; the poet's awareness "bears witness" to the character of reality—bears witness to it subjectively, yet at the same time creates an image of it, and, by doing so, "objectivises" its own awareness. To perceive reality in a certain way is in itself an act which alters the character of reality. "What is objectivity, if not a consensus of different subjectivities?":[6]

I believe that, by dint of being subjective, I am creating an objective type of drama. Perhaps, without even being aware of it, I am really socially conscious.[7]

In these statements, the phenomenological undercurrent which determines much of Ionesco's theoretical argument is clearly apparent. To the phenomenologist, the act of perception is in itself a dual act of creation: the subjective image in the mind is created or modified by an awareness of the outside object; but, at the same time, the object itself is created, or modified, or *given meaning*, by the nature of the awareness which it has itself provoked. For Ionesco, therefore, the very process of perception—let alone that of artistic creation—is literally an *act*: an act which, no less than any other, is the starting-point of an infinite series of repercussions and responsibilities in every sphere. It is not a question of whether one wants or does not want to be "committed"; one *is* committed by the simple fact of being alive, of being conscious. The first of all commitments is existence; the rest are incidental. The solitary is as deeply involved in the ultimate destiny of man as is the Party Member; to join a group, to adhere to a programme is merely a clumsy, noisy, and possibly dangerous way of doing what is inevitable in any case. It is also, perhaps, an easier way—a delegation of responsibility, a form of escapism, a "detachment system," as Madeleine and Choubert realise all too well.[8] In *Le Tueur*, it is the Soldier, the member of the "group," who refuses to participate ("I don't know . . . *I've* got my flowers"),[9] while Bérenger, the very symbol of loneliness and isolation, bears on his shoulders the total responsibility of man:

> You'd think I was frightened, but I'm not. I'm used to being alone . . . I've always been alone. . . . And yet I love the human race, but at a distance. What does that matter, when I'm interested in the fate of mankind? Fact is, I *am* doing something. . . . Doing . . . acting . . . acting, not play-acting, doing![10]

That history is made, not by political movements, nor by the application of carefully-evolved, rationalistic doctrines, but by the imperceptible creative action of the

individual consciousness, is fundamental to Ionesco's
attitude of dissent. It is, admittedly, a romantic attitude;
yet Ionesco's very mistrust of "history," his stress on the
themes of solitude, anguish, and death, is an apt historical
comment upon this particular age—an age in which, in
Professor Schérer's words, "the appearance of new social
structures has confronted the individual with problems
which he cannot solve with his own unaided strength."[11]
For Ionesco, the "historical" (or, for "historical," read
"political") solution of such problems is not merely foredoomed to failure, but, by the operation of a universal
"law of contradiction," is predestined to achieve precisely the opposite of what it sets out to perform. So intense
and deep-rooted is Ionesco's mistrust of the self-adver-
tised "political man" that he resorts to a positively
'pataphysical argument—reminiscent of Rousseau—to
present his case. The individual, in relation to society,
has not one "will," but two: a conscious will to improve
the lot of his fellow-men, and a subconscious *anti*-will
which desires exclusively their destruction:

> No sooner does an idea, a conscious intention, seek to
> realise itself *historically*, than it finds an incarnation in
> its own opposite; it becomes a monstrosity. [. . .] We
> wish the contrary of what we wish. There is a will and
> an anti-will; a wish-for-this, a corresponding anti-
> wish-for-that. And this anti-will is revealed (for we are
> not aware of it, it remains hidden) in the experience
> of *facts*: in the immediate contradiction that it brings
> about. . . .[12]

For Rousseau, it was the *conscious* desire of the individual to realise his own personal interest (*la volonté
particulière*) which constituted the obstacle; yet every
citizen had deep within him a *subconscious* wish for the
general prosperity of the community, and it was this
hidden reflexion of the *volonté générale* which the wise
legislator was concerned to exploit. For Ionesco, the

position is reversed. The conscious will may desire the salvation of mankind; but there is always the all-powerful subconscious to wreak vengeance on the illusion of good intentions. In Ionesco's "Man," there is more than a suspicion of original sin; more than a hint of Manichæism in his philosophy of contradiction. For as long as he remains alone, remains himself, his "will" may dominate his acts; but as soon as he renounces his solitude, as soon as he conforms to the pattern of a class or party, then the secret "anti-will" takes over, and universal devastation is the outcome.

This, then, is the background to Ionesco's unremitting hostility to the notion of "commitment," when commitment involves the conscious acceptance by the individual of a party programme, whose aim is to "reform" the existing state of things. "My Plays make no Claim to Reform the World"[13] is the characteristic title which, echoing the 'Pataphysicians, he once chose for an article published in *Express*. Between "reform" and "revolution" lies all the difference in the world—all the difference between Lenin and Makhnò. The mutual mistrust between Ionesco and his "committed" critics is precisely that between the genuine anarchist and the Left-wing committee-men, who, precisely because they constitute a revolutionary *party*, can no longer pursue the dream of revolution to its logical conclusion.

Far from being a "formalist," a silent supporter of the Right, Ionesco glories in the "subversive" character of his own drama. "The *avant-garde* writer is, as it were, an enemy in the very heart of the city—a city which he is fighting to destroy, against which he is in active revolt. . . ."[14] In fact, there is no such thing as "formalism" in such a context, for to destroy a "formula" is to destroy an ideology, to reveal the absurdity of a jargon is to reveal the absurdity of a whole social structure, of which the logic of language is more than the expression, is indeed the very core and essence. The *political* revolutionary is at best a reformer, altering the appearance of society while leaving intact its inner structure; the artist alone can destroy and refashion the mentality upon which that society is based:

> Science and art have done far more to change thinking than politics have. The real revolution is taking place in the scientists' laboratories and in the artists' studios. Einstein, Oppenheimer, Breton, Kandinsky, Picasso, Pavlov, they're the ones who are really responsible [. . .]. Penicillin and the fight against dipsomania are worth more than politics and a change of government.[15]

In other words, given the true revolution, the "revolution which is a change in mentality,"[16] the corresponding upheaval in social structure will necessarily follow after; by contrast, to impose a social reconstruction without first revolutionising the minds of those who are due to be reconstructed is to coerce the fabric of society against the nature of its own material—a process which can only be achieved by brute force. Ultimately, Ionesco is not so much hostile to "committed" literature as such—after all, "every writer has wanted to make propaganda; the great ones are those who have failed"[17]—as afraid of its results. The assertion that "all ideologies are aggressive, even the most revolutionary,"[18] is one which is not easily contradicted from the evidence of European history over the past fifty years; and over Ionesco's argument there hangs constantly the shadow of Belsen. "A committed theatre is dangerous—exceedingly dangerous. It leads directly to the concentration camp."[19]

But this is not all; for not merely are revolutionary politics, like all politics, "fatal to man," but they are not even, in the deeper sense of the term, revolutionary. Before it can be fashioned into a "programme," an idea must already have been disseminated, popularised, diluted—in other words, bandied about from platform to platform, from committee to committee, until its novelty is tarnished, its subversive violence tamed, its unfamiliarity made acceptable. But by this time, it is no longer revolutionary; it is no longer even alive. "Once an idea has been formulated, it is already dead, and reality has hurried on ahead."[20] Politics, more than any other aspect of the "conformist" society in which we live, feeds on platitudes, for no idea, unless it be already dead as mutton (from the artist's point of view) can figure on a "programme" without scorching a hole in the paper. Political fingers are easily burnt by the fire of live ideas. Consequently, for a writer to harness his art to the politics of a party is to surrender his right to be revolutionary and to chain his living language to the senseless cadavers of words which have already lost half, if not all, their meaning. And to accept a form of language, a way of thought which is already out-of-date and platitudinous is to betray the truth, to distort reality—in short, to propagate a *lie*.

In the summer of 1958, Ionesco was soundly taken to task for these and other related ideas by Kenneth Tynan, Orson Welles, Philip Toynbee and others, in a series of articles which appeared in the *Observer*.[21] The essence of Tynan's criticism was that Ionesco's unappeasable mistrust of *a priori* political value-judgments had led him to divorce his art *entirely* from its social context, and to produce a subjective, "formalistic" type of drama (cp. Arnold Wesker, Shelagh Delaney, etc.), in which his own, purely private obsessions and inner preoccupations were puffed up, all sheathed in a cascade of glittering linguistic fireworks, into a sort of cheap and spurious "universality." Yet a drama which rejected ideology, Tynan suggested, was at once narrow, dangerous, and hollow: narrow because it could have only a limited, "*élite*" appeal; dangerous because, by its "formalism," it suggested that all was well in the world of "You-never-had-it-so-good"; hollow because, by professing to despise "man as a social animal," it could offer no more than a partial and incomplete portrait of reality:

Art and ideology often interact on each other; but the main fact is that both spring from a common source. Both draw on human experience to explain mankind to itself; both attempt, in very different ways, to assemble a coherence from seemingly unrelated phenomena; both stand guard for us against Chaos.[22]

—to which Ionesco retorted: "Social man is hell; other people are hell; if only one could do without them!"[23] . . . and the controversy became slightly embittered.

To dismiss this controversy as a simple misunderstanding of Ionesco's purpose, or even as a (mistaken) attempt to judge Ionesco in terms of Brecht, is perhaps to oversimplify the problem. The argument reflects a conflict of tradition, as well as a clash of historical experience; and the whole attitude towards Ionesco in England and America is coloured by the implications of the debate. Ionesco has been recognised in the English theatre almost as widely as in France—but for rather different reasons. It takes an audience brought up against a background of Cartesian logic to accept Ionesco's anti-logic at its face value; the English empirical tradition looks rather for the practical implications—and sometimes finds them. For English audiences, it is necessary that the unexplainable should be explained, should even help in explaining something else (compare the productions of *Rhinocéros* by Orson Welles in London and by Jean-Louis Barrault in Paris);[24] and when it fails to do so, they feel that they have been deceived. Not that Ionesco deceives them *in his plays*, for his drama is so complex, contains so many threads, that (to take an instance), *Les Chaises* has been interpreted either as a study in the breakdown of "classical psychology," or, alternatively, as a straightforward and realistic psychiatric case-history ("*folie à deux*") in dramatic form. Similarly, *La Leçon* has been taken as a "myth"—a full-scale political allegory of a "people" oppressed by a "Dictator," of its desperate and

futile attempt at revolt (the Girl-Student's toothache),
and of its eventual repression.[25] "Apparently," Ionesco
himself remarks somewhere, "one can get a lesson out of
anything—even out of *La Leçon*." But the shock comes
when, having allowed his audience their rationalistic
interpretation as they sat in the theatre, he then denies
them the slightest right to such Anglo-Saxon self-in-
dulgence in his theoretical commentaries. *La Leçon* is an
allegory of nothing; it is just . . . a lesson. Even *Jacques*—
apparently a political and social satire on the bourgeoisie
—is "totally uncommitted." In a way—given the contrasting national attitudes—both the antagonists are
right: Tynan to insist that the play should *mean* what it
does, or might, or conceivably could be made to mean;
Ionesco to retort that all meaning is subordinate to
absurdity:

> The theatre, like all art, must serve no utilitarian
> purpose; the theatre is not *engagement* but *dégagement*;
> none the less, this "disengagement," this alienation,
> this forgetfulness of self, this violent separation from
> the utilitarian world, is a usefulness *without which we
> cannot live.* . . .[26]

The question, however, as put by the English side of
the controversy, is wrongly presented: the argument is
not whether Ionesco should or should not be committed,
for Ionesco—as I have tried to show—*is* committed, and
the argument is fruitless. The problem is to see precisely
to what he is committed, and in what way. He is committed to "Man," to "the Left," to revolution, to anarchy
even: but he is *not* committed to Marx or to Marxism, to the Trotskyists, the Socialists, the F.L.N., or the
New Left. Whereas, in the English view—or in the
Sartrian view—he should be; for revolutionary dreams
divorced from political action are nothing, are worse
than nothing, a snare, a delusion, a gift handed on a
silver platter to the ogres of the Establishment.

But here, between these irreconcilable views, the actual experience of history intervenes. English political history has on the whole been kind to the principle of opposition; the English intellectual who dissents from the accepted platitudes of the Establishment risks seldom more than a certain notoriety, a certain amount of defamation and vituperation, a couple of stormy scenes in Parliament or in the police-court, a few mass-meetings, protest-marches —and ultimately he stands to gain a measure of adjustment in the law. In such a context, a greater or lesser degree of opposition is scarcely less than a duty consequent upon the possession of intelligence. In France, the background, although different, is still comparable. In the absence of a deeply-rooted parliamentary tradition, the intellectual's responsibility is from the first more sharply focused on *activity*—on party warfare (still largely verbal), on propaganda, speech-making and organisation. But Ionesco's experience is neither French nor English, but fundamentally *Nazi*: Nazi Roumania, Nazi-occupied France, with the politics of the post-war "People's Republic" in Bucharest thrown in for good measure. And the quintessential lesson of this experience is that parties which begin as ideological minorities will necessarily develop—under contemporary European conditions—into dictatorial police states, so that the final condition of the unhappy citizen is infinitely worse than the first. Admittedly, the poet's first duty is to "impose his universe"[27]—but to do so from within, never from without. To codify this "inner universe," to formulate it in the neat phrases of an ideology, to cease to be a "witness" and to become an "orator," is directly to hasten the advent of the concentration camp, the mass-execution, and the pogrom.

And, indeed, the hidden theme of much of Ionesco's drama is precisely this: the denunciation of the police state as the final, most nefarious incarnation of the "bourgeois" mind. Concerning the various Communist

régimes in Europe, he has little to say—an isolated out-
burst of indignation at the time of the Pasternak "affair,"[28]
a few generalised criticisms of Marxism (of no great
weight) in *Pages de journal*,[29] an occasional *boutade* in the
vein: "Nothing is more conducive to pessimism than the
obligation to eschew pessimism . . . or go to gaol!";[30] and,
indeed, in certain Communist countries, notably in
Poland and in Jugoslavia, Ionesco's drama has enjoyed
a quite phenomenal success. But where Fascism is concerned (not forgetting the crypto-Fascism of the petty,
would-be Nazis, the bullies, the *agents de police*, the
concierges), his pen can never be bitter enough nor "committed" enough to express the fullness of his fear, contempt, and hatred. From *Le Maître* and *Victimes du devoir*,
by way of *Tueur sans gages*, to *Rhinocéros*, Ionesco's drama
is an implacable diatribe against the oppression and
poison of the Nazi state; the nightmare which absorbs
all other nightmares is that of Adolf Hitler.

The grotesque and horrifying episode of La Mère Pipe
and her goose-stepping regiment of thugs in *Le Tueur*
needs no comment; but some critics (especially in
England) have been less aware of the implications of
Rhinocéros. The fell disease of "rhinoceritis" is the condemnation, not of *any* ideology to which man may feel the
urge to conform, but specifically of the *Nazi* ideology.
Not that the allusion is in any way historical; Fascism is
far from belonging exclusively to the past, and indeed,
the urgency of the play, the menacing tempo of its
dramatic rhythm, makes it very much a warning to be
heeded here and now. The average audience is all too
eager to find any excuse not to apply a dramatic moral to
itself, and it was probably in an attempt to avoid the pit-
fall of "history" that Ionesco deliberately omitted all
references which might associate the drama with a
specific place and epoch. Having avoided the particular,
however, he found himself caught out on the general; for
all too many of the critics, their safe refuge in history

being denied to them, have retaliated by turning the play
into an *abstraction*—a "universal parable" on the subject
of "conformism." Universal it may be; but when "universality" is used as an excuse for making oneself deaf to
a call to action, then it is time to restate the particular.

The theory that *Rhinocéros*, in its initial conception, is
a deliberate onslaught against Fascism is borne out, not
only by Ionesco's own occasional assertions, but by the
evidence of the origins of the play as such. One of the
recurrent themes of *Rhinocéros* is the conflict between
the "ideal of civilisation" and the "ideal of nature":

JEAN: After all, rhinoceroses are living creatures the
    same as us; they've got as much right to life as we
    have!
BÉRENGER: As long as they don't destroy ours in the
    process. You must admit the difference in mentality.
JEAN: Are you under the impression that our way of
    life is superior?
BÉRENGER: Well at any rate, we have our own moral
    standards which I consider incompatible with the
    standards of these animals.
JEAN: Moral standards! I'm sick of moral standards!
    We need to go beyond moral standards!
BÉRENGER: What would you put in their place?
JEAN: Nature!
BÉRENGER: Nature?
JEAN: Nature has its own laws. Morality's against
    Nature.
BÉRENGER: Are you suggesting we replace our moral
    laws by the law of the jungle?
JEAN: It would suit me, suit me fine.
BÉRENGER: You say that. But deep down, no one . . .
JEAN: We've got to build our life on new foundations.
    We must get back to primeval integrity. . . .[31]

In this passage (as in the later arguments between
Bérenger and Dudard) the rhinoceros incarnates the

dream of simplifying the complexities of an over-civilised society, of a return to "natural innocence" and to a "state of nature" in which the degeneracy of modern man will be finally purged and redeemed. But, to Ionesco, it is precisely this glorification of nature which constitutes by far and away the most dangerous aspect of the Nazi ideology—dangerous because it may have a quite genuine appeal to the over-civilised mentality. In an essay written some ten years earlier, we find the same theme worked out in detail; this time, however, with the allusions made plain and the missing references filled in. This article (unfortunately unpublished) is entitled: "Un Témoignage faux: La Vingt-cinquième Heure," and is a highly critical review of C. Virgil Gheorghiu's popular novel, *The Twenty-fifth Hour*.[32] In many ways, it may be considered the germ of the later play. Among other fashionable intellectual pursuits, declares Ionesco, is that of denouncing the "oppressive automatism of a robot machine-age." But this is an error; the machine, on the whole, is beneficial to man, is at least a product of *civilisation*; even the automatism and impersonality of bureaucracy has its advantages, precisely *because* it is impersonal. The real danger lies not in the robot, but

in the automatism of passions and of evil instincts, the biological and physiological automatism of the Fascist beast [. . .]. The automatism of the machine is *not* dangerous; it is the sub-human automatisms which are [. . .]. Nazism likewise was opposed to the "machine age" and to "abstractions"; Nazism was this and nothing else—the revolt of nature and of the instincts of the brute against civilisation, to the point where the "man of the future," as Hitler wished to see him and was prepared to fashion him, was the *wild beast*. What, in point of fact, was the S.S.? A machine? No, rather a stupid bird of prey, with the brain, it goes without saying, of a bird. . . .[33]

—while, in a later passage from the same work, one comes across a sentence which, in one neat phrase, summarises the whole of the plot on which *Rhinocéros* is built:

Nature against mind—there you have the whole of Nazism.[34]

This, obviously, is not the total content of *Rhinocéros*, which, like all Ionesco's plays, is extremely complex in its thematic structure; but it is certainly the *leitmotiv*, the initial inspiration, without which the play would not have been written at all. The picture of the progressive transformation of man into rhinoceros (with all that this implies) is as explicit and as "committed" a statement as one could wish: a warning of the most peremptory order against the ever-present menace of the Fascist "appeal to instinct."

On the other hand, the superficial impression that Ionesco's theatre by and large is a-political is strengthened, not only by the dramatist's own deliberately provocative assertions, but also by the fact that his satire rarely touches upon identifiable details; most of it is concerned with issues so broad (the ultimate bankruptcy of the bourgeois ideology, etc.), that its immediate social or political implications are lost sight of in the general chaotic dissolution of accepted standards which ensues. Not that even Ionesco can resist letting off an occasional squib—the Swastika arm-band in *La Leçon*, as the Professor proceeds to dispose of his forty corpses; the drunken American soldier in *Amédée*, who, threatened with the Military Police, retorts simply (in English!): "Military Police? I belong to it!";[35] the bloated patron of the arts in *Le Tableau* exploiting and humiliating his toadying little painter—even allusions of a more personal kind, such as the readily-identifiable trio of critics in *L'Impromptu*,[36] or the oblique reference to M. Morvan-Lebesque in *Le Tueur*.[37] But, of all the plays, perhaps *L'Avenir* alone relies on this sort of irony to any considerable degree. On the other hand, there are two broad and constantly-reiterated themes which carry strong political implications, and which, when they occur finally in combination, contrive to make *Rhinocéros* one of the most significant political plays of the twentieth century.

The first of these is the idea that the forces of social order which hold the state together—the police, the civil service, the army—are the highest incarnation of the principle of "logical necessity," as conceived by the bourgeois mind. But once the illusion of logic has disintegrated, as in Ionesco's view of the world it has, then nothing remains of these forces but an empty shell. Just as meaning has departed from language, leaving only a hollow crust of platitudes, just as the concept of a rational justice has evaporated, leaving only the echoing reverberations of legalistic formulæ, so likewise the controlling forces of society have lost their *raison d'être*. A police-force is just as gratuitous in a society without justice as an army is in a world of hydrogen bombs. When all clues are meaningless (and this is one of the problems of *Victimes du devoir*), how should a detective set about detecting? But, even when deprived of meaning, the shells of authority still remain; indeed, like all inanimate objects, not merely remain, but proliferate at the expense of man; and *power without sense* is the most evil, the most dangerous phenomenon with which poor "modern man" can be confronted.

The theme of senseless brutality substituted for order and justice is found everywhere in Ionesco, but above all in *Victimes du devoir* and in *Le Tueur*. The beating-up of the Old Man and of the Soldier-with-the-Bunch-of-Flowers, followed by the total moral disintegration of Bérenger when ordered to "show his papers,"[38] are merely the logical development of the "brain-washing" sequence which forms the central episode of *Victimes du devoir*. It is significant that whereas Ionesco's soldiers tend to be harmless, even despicable, individuals, the civilian authorities (who incarnate the very concept of social logic) are menacing and evil. "Everything will have to be changed," declares Bérenger; "first we must start by reforming the police force."[39] Even the Fireman of *La Cantatrice* is vaguely threatening; more so the Concierge of *Le Nouveau Locataire*; more so still (although apparently benevolent) is the City Architect of *Le Tueur*. For the Architect (who is also the *Commissaire de Police*) symbolises, not merely power without sense in a disintegrating social order, but also "the Administration"—that insubstantial father-figure whose authority alone can satisfy the sub-conscious of the Common Man. The "Administration" is not so much menacing in itself (although it appears so to both Choubert and Amédée), as dangerous on account of what might happen should it prove illusory. Relying upon the all-wisdom of Authority, the common man can shrug off his responsibilities, confident that this intangible *something* will accept the burden in his stead, and, in return for surrendered liberty, give justice, order, and a comfortable quietude. For such is the principle of Social Contract—that scintillatingly logical pillar of the bour-geois state. "We ought," says Jean, upon the appearance of the first Rhinoceros, "to protest to the Town Council! What's the Council there for?"[40] But, in Ionesco's world, as poor Dany had already discovered, "the Civil Service [*l'Administration*] is *not* responsible";[41] there is no all-wise, all-provident "Town Council" to guarantee the order of society, because there *is* no order in society. The Social Contract is repudiated, and willy-nilly man must take back his liberty, and manage it as best he can. The menace, therefore, which emanates both from the Police and from the Architect is of a similar order: in the general disintegration of the bourgeois system, rational discipline, now void of meaning, is replaced by *force* emanating absurdly from the "automatism of instinct," while, for the victim, the last redress, the ultimate court of appeal, has vanished into smoke. In such a context, even to *try* to apply the criteria and conventions of social morality is totally absurd. Bourgeois society has lost its reason for existence, and henceforward (until the time of that *inner revolution* which is destined to "transform his mentality") the life of bourgeois man is destined to be "solitary, poor, nasty, brutish, and short."

But man is not merely betrayed by the forces which incarnate the bourgeois-rational ideal of society; he is more directly and more fatally betrayed by reason itself. This is the second general theme of *Rhinocéros*. *Rhinocéros* is more than a simple study of the herd-instinct; the point that Ionesco has striven to make is that the "herd" (the mad rush of Dostoevskian "possessed") is no longer composed of the old "unthinking mass." Ours is, all in all, a *thinking* civilisation; the modern mob is not a rabble of *sans-culottes*, but a mutinied regiment of reasoners and logicians, of all those who exploit the illusion of logic to justify the unjustifiable. The danger of the illusion is that the same type of logical argument which, in the field of abstract speculation, exploits logic and reason to disguise the non-logical essence of reality, can be used, and is used, on the political level, to justify any form of oppression, atrocious cruelty or exploitation—in brief, any variety of Fascism—that may happen to come into existence. This, ultimately, is the theme to which Ionesco is committed: the betrayal of man by his own intellect.

Rhinocéros is fundamentally an analysis of this betrayal. The problem is not "What is Fascism?" but "How does a rational and civilised nation come to accept the Fascist ideal?" And Ionesco's answer is that, accustomed to veil all reality behind the illusion of logic, the bourgeois mind has come to rely on reason to supply an *a posteriori* justification for whatever phenomenon may happen to arise. How a phenomenon achieves existence (how the first rhinoceros appeared) is not Ionesco's problem; it is the reactions of the thinking mind *after* the appearance which fascinate and horrify him. Faced with the sudden crisis, the first reaction is to disguise the fact of reality with meaningless words and platitudes; then to side-track the significant issue altogether (". . . for it is possible that since its first appearance, the rhinoceros may have lost one of its horns, and that the first and second transit were still made by a single beast . . .");[42] next, to shift the responsibility on to the "Town Council"; and finally to deny that the phenomenon had ever occurred at all.

Confronted ultimately, however, with incontrovertible evidence of the fact, the second series of reactions is more sinister. The real evil begins with M. Botard, the "Brechtian," the "committed propagandist," obsessed with his resolve to discover "the whys and the wherefores of the whole business":

> I know my own mind. I'm not content to simply state that a phenomenon exists. I make it my business to understand it and explain it.[43]

But, as Sukhanov remarks somewhere, à propos of the Menshevik theorist, Martov, "in politics, to understand too much is inadmissible, *parce que comprendre, c'est pardonner.*" In the same way, in Ionesco's context, to "understand" and to "explain" a phenomenon is merely a disguised way of justifying its existence, a trick, once again, to divert the awareness of the mind from the terror of the fact to some nice, comforting and totally irrelevant consideration. Once the fatal assumption has been made that, in a world supposedly logical, each and every existing phenomenon must partake of this necessary logicality, the harm is done. If it exists, therefore it *must* be the necessary result of a given and ascertainable cause; and since the law of cause-and-effect is inescapable, the phenomenon is inescapable likewise. Rationalism, in other words, is merely fatalism disguised. The necessity of the phenomenon *justifies* its existence, and what is logically justified cannot logically be opposed. Worse: for the logical mind soon grows so exclusively preoccupied with demonstrating the necessity, that it contrives secretly to do what it has been aspiring to do all along: namely, to lose sight of the phenomenon altogether, to disregard its implications, and to hide reality behind a smoke-screen of argument. M. Botard himself having (inevitably) become a rhinoceros, the thread is taken up by M. Dudard:

> My dear Bérenger, one must always make an effort to understand. And in order to understand a phenomenon and its effects you need to work back to the initial causes, by honest intellectual effort. We must try to do this because, after all, we are thinking beings. I haven't yet succeeded, as I told you, and I don't know if I shall succeed. But in any case, one has to start out favourably disposed—or at least, impartial; one has to keep an open mind—that's essential to a scientific mentality. Everything is logical. To understand is to justify.[44]

This, then, is the final betrayal of intellect. Because it has accepted, lock, stock, and barrel, the illusion of logic, reason has allowed itself to degenerate into the slave and sycophant of facts; as the facts proliferate, so reason is progressively "victimised" by the material world, while at the same time it contrives to hide its impotence and degradation under the flamboyant banners of "understanding," "tolerance for others," and "scientific detachment." Bérenger alone resists the general infatuation: his salvation, his "originality" (like that of Amédée) lies in his positive acceptance of the irrational; he alone, in his *naïveté*, receives the facts for what they are, instead of striving to demonstrate their "logical necessity," thus obliterating the significance of the facts themselves. In such a context, reason is no longer "wisdom," but "oriental fatalism"; if reason—*any* reason—can serve to justify the Nazi creed, then reason by that alone stands finally condemned. The principles of rationalism are inadequate to deal with the world of Hitler and Hiroshima, and Bérenger's despairing cry is hauntingly significant:

Well, in that case, I . . . I *refuse to think!*[45]

Ultimately, politics are rational; and therefore the political solution *cannot* be the final solution in an irrational world. Like Bérenger, who feels himself "responsible for everything that happens . . . involved . . . unable to be indifferent,"[46] Ionesco is deeply committed to the cause of man. But man, as he sees him, is not fundamentally a political animal, because the political solution, *even when achieved*, will still leave the eternal, the essential problems unanswered. Utopia *may* lie ahead— but what happens after? Ionesco is committed—urgently —to averting the cataclysms towards which present politics seem unerringly to be heading; he is committed —less urgently—to bringing about "a world where economic worries are a thing of the past, a universe without mystery where everything runs smoothly";[47] but his ultimate commitment is to the solution of the problems of man in the world *beyond* Utopia. It is not true that he is "neutral" (as Orson Welles suggests) in the conflict of ideologies; but both as a dramatist and as a philosopher, he is possessed of that "thirst for the absolute" which must, for all time, fail to be satisfied with the temporary shifts and compromises of practical politics. As a dramatist, because the problems of politics, like those of Molière, are "in the last analysis relatively secondary, sometimes sad, certainly even dramatic, but never tragic: for they can all be resolved";[48] as a philosopher, because the political solution can never go beyond Utopia, whereas it is precisely with the coming of Utopia that "we shall see that this solves nothing, indeed that our problems are only just beginning."[49] Even in Utopia, man will still be faced with death, with boredom, with absurdity; and the confrontation will be all the more intolerable for taking place in a universe devoid of wars and crises and distractions, amid the boundless silence and "emptiness of a world without metaphysics."[50]

To Ionesco, man's isolation is fundamental. No mass-meeting, no communal parade with banners, be it a million strong, will alleviate for one instant the obsessive loneliness which springs from the simple awareness of death. If there *is* an escape from such loneliness, it can only lie in another *kind* of community—a community whose bonds are deeper, more intimate than the superficial links of Welfare economics:

The truly social, the authentic community, is *extra-social*. To reach the heart of the matter, we must discover a broader, profounder type of society—that of our common anguish, revealed to us through our desires, our unfathomable longings. The entire history of the world is governed by longings, by anguishes such as these, and political activity has never succeeded in realising it otherwise than imperfectly, partially. No society has ever succeeded in abolishing such sadness; no political programme can ever deliver us from the *malaise* of existence, from our fear of death, from our thirst for the absolute. It is the nature of man which dictates the nature of society, and not *vice versa*.[51]

REFERENCES

1. Paul Guth, *Le Naïf aux quarante enfants*, Paris 1954, p. 62.
2. "Entretien," p. 12.
3. "Finalement," p. 2.
4. "L'Invraisemblable," p. 1.
5. *Ibid.*
6. "Entretien," pp. 12–13.
7. "Finalement," p. 2.
8. N.R.F., I. 178–9 (II. 267–9).
9. N.R.F., II. 152 (III. 88–9).
10. N.R.F., II. 159 (III. 95–6).
11. Jacques Schérer, "L'Evolution de Ionesco," p. 95.
12. "Le Bloc-notes d'Eugène Ionesco," p. 2.
13. "Mes pièces ne prétendent pas sauver le monde," p. 8.
14. "E.I.o.f.," pp. 176–7.

15. N.R.F., II. 144 (III. 82).
16. "Le Cœur n'est pas sur la main," p. 263.
17. "Finalement," p. 2.
18. Quoted by P. Sarisson in *Aux Ecoutes*, 16 Jan. 1959.
19. Lerminier, "Dialogue avec Ionesco," p. 53.
20. "E.I.o.f.," pp. 176–7.
21. *Observer* (London), 22 and 29 Jun., 6 and 13 Jul. 1958.
22. *Observer*, 13 Jul. 1958.
23. "Le Cœur n'est pas sur la main," p. 266. This article, Ionesco's final reply to his English critics, was sent to the *Observer*, but was never published by that paper.
24. Cp. Dorothy Knowles, "Ionesco's Rhinoceroses," pp. 35–9.
25. Pierre-Aimé Touchard, "Eugène Ionesco a réinventé les mythes du théâtre," p. 2.
26. "Théâtre et anti-théâtre," p. 151.
27. "E.I.o.f.," pp. 190–1.
28. "Celui qui ose ne pas haïr . . . ," pp. 1–2.
29. "Pages de journal," p. 221.
30. Frédéric Towarnicki, "Ionesco des *Chaises* vides . . . ," p. 12.
31. *Rhinocéros*, pp. 126–7 (*Plays*, IV. 66–7).
32. Virgil Gheorghiu, *La Vingt-cinquième Heure*, Fr. tr. by Monique Saint-Côme (who originally introduced Ionesco to Nicolas Bataille, and thus was indirectly responsible for the first production of *La Cantatrice*), Paris 1949, Engl. tr. by Rita Eldon, London 1950.
33. *Un Témoignage faux*, MS (in the possession of Eugène Ionesco), pp. 12–13.
34. *Op. cit.*, p. 13.
35. N.R.F., I. 298 (II. 217).
36. Bernard Dort, J.-J. Gautier, Roland Barthes; see "Finalement," p. 1.
37. N.R.F., II. 109 (III. 52, footnote).
38. N.R.F., II.153–5(III. 89–91).
39. N.R.F., II. 159 (III. 95).
40. *Rhinocéros*, p. 30 (*Plays*, IV. 14).
41. N.R.F., II. 83 (III. 29).
42. *Rhinocéros*, p. 67 (*Plays*, IV. 36).
43. *Rhinocéros*, p. 104 (*Plays*, IV. 54).
44. *Rhinocéros*, p. 158 (*Plays*, IV. 83).
45. *Rhinocéros*, p. 161 (*Plays*, IV. 85).
46. *Rhinocéros*, p. 149 (*Plays*, IV. 78).
47. "The World of Eugène Ionesco," p. 46.
48. "D. Th.," p. 6.
49. "The World of Eugène Ionesco," p. 46.
50. *Op. cit.*, p. 47.
51. "Ionesco à l'heure anglaise," p. 133.

CHAPTER VI

THE SEARCH FOR MEANING

Ionesco is a creative writer—and few indeed are those creative writers who have the gift of fruitfully criticising others. As a school-teacher in Rumania, it is to be guessed that his courses on the greater French classics were probably inspiring rather than conventional. He himself tells how, on one occasion in 1934 or thereabouts, he published a scathing, a positively vitriolic attack on the poets Anghezi and Barbu, and on the novelist Petresco. These figures being firmly ensconced in the Pantheon of Rumanian literature, there ensued no little scandal; "there were articles in learned journals, there were refutations, there was even a public debate with repercussions." Some two months later, he published a second series of articles, "some five or six in all," once more discussing these same three authors, but this time extolling them to high heaven. The initial scandal, as may be inferred, was nothing to the torrent of abuse unleashed by the second stage of this Hegelian dialectic, and "a promising career as a critic was irretrievably ruined."[1] At the time, this was possibly little more than an undergraduate escapade; Ionesco himself explained it as "an experiment preparatory to writing an article entitled *NO!*, and dealing with the identity of opposites." In retrospect, however, the incident takes on some significance. "All I was trying to do was to show that it is exceedingly difficult to lay down the law about a work of art [. . .]. The work of art is untranslatable; it *cannot* be translated into any other language."[2]

This is of course true of all art, but it is more especially true of abstract art, to which Ionesco's drama constantly aspires. In the absence of any *a priori* concept of beauty, such as that which held sway in France in the seventeenth century, it is difficult to judge a work of art, save either in formal terms, or else in terms of whatever aspect of "reality" (visual, social, ideological) that work may "represent"; but when—as is the case with abstract painting—the work categorically renounces all attempts to "represent" any aspect of reality which can be apprehended through the senses, there remains no criterion save the inherent, formal structure of the work itself. In other words, although abstract art is not necessarily "formalistic," the *criterion* of such art must inevitably be so, since there is no other criterion which is relevant. Such at least is Ionesco's argument—and here again he comes into collision with Kenneth Tynan and the English "committed" school, for whom such "formalistic" criticism counts as a mere academic exercise, and for whom the social or political implications of the work, even when hidden or wholly negative, must find pride of place. For the political situation of the world is desperate, and to step aside from the arena, deliberately to turn one's back on the issues at stake, is by implication to give one's assent to policies and values which may prove fatal. As Orson Welles most categorically asserts: "An artist must either confirm the values of his society; or he must challenge them."[3] Ionesco, as I have tried to show, is very far from wishing to opt out of the problems of his century; none the less, having chosen to express his convictions in the form of dramas rather than as political pamphlets, he claims the right to have his work considered on its own terms—*i.e.* not as a manifesto in this cause or in that, but as *theatre*.

By and large, French critics have been prepared to grant him this without much argument. It is significant that *L'Impromptu de l'Alma*—a long-winded and unsatisfactory piece of satire which none the less contrives to drive home its point—makes hardly any reference to the problems of "committedness" and "social responsibility" which so deeply preoccupy the active empiricists of England. In France, apart from a certain amount of total misunderstanding and undisguised contempt from the orthodox pundits—Jean-Jacques Gautier, for instance (of *Le Figaro*), or Robert Kemp (of *Le Monde*)[4]—Ionesco's main adversaries have been those who have criticised his drama on *formal* grounds. The point that Bartholoméus I, II and III all make is that Ionesco's theatre fails to abide by the principles of "correct" dramatic construction—whether this be classical, Brechtian, or Bernsteinian—and therefore cannot be considered valid as a form of art:

BARTHOLOMÉUS II: You admit your mistakes?

IONESCO [*with an effort*]: Why yes, Gentlemen . . . yes . . . my ignorance, my mistakes . . . I'm very sorry . . . please forgive me . . . all I ask is to be taught what's right. . . . [*He beats his chest.*] Mea culpa! Mea maxima culpa!

BARTHOLOMÉUS III: Is this sincere?

IONESCO: Oh yes . . . I swear it is! . . .

BARTHOLOMÉUS II: No sinner but should find mercy.

IONESCO: Oh thank you . . . thank you. . . . How good you are, Gentlemen!

BARTHOLOMÉUS I [*to Bartholoméus II*]: Don't give way to the temptation of goodness! We'll soon see if he's really sincere.

IONESCO: Oh yes, I am sincere.

BARTHOLOMÉUS III: Let him prove it then, by his works.

BARTHOLOMÉUS I: Not by his works.

BARTHOLOMÉUS II: His works don't count.

BARTHOLOMÉUS I: It's only his theories that count.

BARTHOLOMÉUS II: What he *thinks* of his work.

BARTHOLOMÉUS I: For the work itself . . .

BARTHOLOMÉUS II: Doesn't exist . . .

BARTHOLOMÉUS I: Except in what one says about it . . .[5]

This preoccupation with the theories of art and the

principles of beauty is highly characteristic of French criticism; and despite the fact that Ionesco reproaches the three Bartholoméus with having substituted absolute for relative values, with having dressed them up in cabbalistic language, and with having sought, by wielding them, to "govern artistic creation even to the point of tyranny,"[6] none the less, even the attitudes of a Gautier or a Kemp are less foreign to him than those of a Welles or a Tynan. For it is Welles's contention that the critic has every right to judge the work of art in terms of what it is *not*, because its very deficiencies may be directly or indirectly dangerous to the survival of humanity; whereas it is Ionesco's contention that the work should be judged exclusively in terms of what it *is*—even if the verdict is unfavourable. "The critic," concludes the *Impromptu*, "should describe and not prescribe."[7]

It is too early yet, obviously, to talk about any well-defined trends in Ionesco criticism, other than those which have just been mentioned. The early plays were greeted with a cry of bafflement which, while not by any means always hostile, added little but confusion:

I learnt that I had talent: a little, a lot, a cartload, none at all; that I had a sense of humour, that I was born without one; that I was a master of the unexpected, that I possessed the temperament of a mystic; that my plays had metaphysical overtones; that (in another's view) I was by temperament a realist, a psychologist, a notable observer of the human heart, and that my future development should lie in this direction; that I was a formless writer; that my writing had form, was sharply-defined; that my vocabulary was poor; that my vocabulary was rich; that I was an implacable critic of contemporary society; that the greatest weakness of my theatre lay in my failure to denounce the social injustices and the disorders of the Establishment; I was sharply accused of being anti-

H

social; I learnt further that I lacked the gift of poetry, and that this was serious because "without poetry there can be no drama"; that I was a poet, and that this was desperately serious because "what on earth is the sense of poetry?"; that my plays were too consciously contrived, too intellectual and cold; or, on the contrary, that they were primitive, unsophisticated, elemental; that I was systematic, desiccated, devoid of imagination; that I had failed to canalise the excess of my imagination, which was eager, unbounded and undisciplined, and that—far from being desiccated and ascetic as I should be—I was a garrulous chatterbox; that what was interesting about me was that I belonged to the *chosiste* school of dramatists; "Accessories are out of place on the stage," thundered another, "it's bad theatre. What counts is the text"; Yes, it does; No, it doesn't; yes, it does; no, it doesn't . . .[8]

This neatly satirical *résumé* sums up fairly enough the confusion of criticism up to 1955 or shortly after. Nor, during this period, were the spectators particularly numerous; Ionesco's reputation remained still to be made. On Whit Sunday, 1950, the audience at the Théâtre des Noctambules consisted of three people only—but they happened to be Armand Salacrou, Raymond Queneau, and Roger Vitrac! From 1956 onward, however, when Ionesco began to be felt as a serious influence in the theatre, the critics began to sort themselves out gradually into two fairly distinct categories: one (the lesser) seeking to find a specific meaning, first for one play, then for another; the second (the more important), concerned to interpret Ionesco's *intentions*, as revealed in his drama, in terms of the general preoccupations of all thinkers and artists of our time.

The effort of trying to "explain" a given play is almost foredoomed to failure. That the plays have a significance is beyond question. "Ionesco's drama is everything, anything, what you will—save one thing, a game, an intellectual pastime";[9] but whether that significance can be expressed in *precise conceptual terms*, or indeed in *any* terms other than those of the play itself, is doubtful. The dramatic form, for Ionesco, is not one of a number of possible alternatives; it is *the* form, the only form which can express his concept, because the visual image, the gesture, the action, the interplay of dialogue and silence, are as essential to his meaning as are the words themselves.[10] The effectiveness of the plays does not depend upon their rational so much as on their sensual and emotional impact. Saroyan's verdict, that "works of art such as these seem wholly inexplicable at first sight, whereas after a while they grow more inexplicable still,"[11] is not a condemnation, nor is it intended to be; it is a plain statement of fact. Once again, the parallel with abstract painting is enlightening: to ask of Ben Nicholson or Kandinsky "what he means" by this or that is a question which itself has no conceivable meaning; the only way the artist's meaning can be expressed is the way in which it has been expressed already—in the painting. What the spectator makes of it is, of course, a different matter altogether—but here again Ionesco's attitude is categoric:

My audience is completely free to make its own interpretation [. . .]. I cannot anticipate it in any way. I have no right to do so. For either the significance of the play is clear—in which case I have nothing to say —or else it is not—in which case the play is a failure.[12]

The game of "hunting for meanings" is therefore doubly dangerous: dangerous because to reduce a given scene to other terms is actively to distort it, or at least to weaken it appreciably; dangerous also because, once a single aspect of the play (the conceptual aspect) is detached from its general context, almost any significance can be grafted on to it, depending entirely on the preoccupations of the annotator. Thus *La Cantatrice* has been

variously interpreted as a parody of the theatre as an
art-form, or specifically as a parody of the commercial
theatre, or as a critique of the petty-bourgeoisie, or as a
jab at the English, or as a commentary on the Surrealists,
or on the logical positivists, or even as an attack on the
unfortunate *Méthode Assimil* as a technique for mastering
foreign languages. Marc Beigbeder, who sagely remarks
at one point, "A little bird told me that it is unwise to ask
Ionesco exactly what he *means*,"[13] none the less (in the
same article) succumbs to temptation, and "explains" the
Corpse in *Amédée* as "the living corpse of what was, or
might have been, or should have been, their love—a
corpse that both he and she have murdered, robbed
suddenly of life through not knowing how to love each
other, and which now exacts its revenge. . . ."[14] Pierre-
Aimé Touchard finds "myths" and "allegories" in every
play,[15] while for Jacques Lemarchand, *La Leçon* (Touchard's "allegory" of national revolt against dictatorship) is
a fable concerning the invincible ignorance and stupidity
of certain female university students who—it seems—
would rather die than actually *learn* anything.[16] To the
psychologically-minded, *La Leçon* can be a study of the
"power-complex" or incipient megalomania which is
(apparently) common to all those who indulge in the
teaching profession, while *Victimes du devoir* can be taken
as a dramatic illustration of Freud on dreams, or a satire on
the Oedipus-complex—or, for that matter, as a working-
out of Hegelian dialectic. The Killer's knife is death, or non-
communication, or the frustration of bourgeois society, or
the failure of logic, or the corruption of the French (or
Rumanian) police; while *Rhinocéros*, of course, is a satire
on Fascism, or Communism, or Trade-Unionism (M.
Botard), or Big Business (M. Papillon) or (in the absence of
further evidence one way or the other) anything you please.

   In the almost total absence of any "academic" studies
(the determining of Ionesco's exact relationship with
other dramatists, etc.),[17] by far the most fruitful criticism

to date is that which has followed the path of philo-sophical speculation. Critics such as Marcel Brion, J. S. Doubrovsky, André Muller, Jacques Schérer, and, above all, Jean Vannier, instead of attempting to extract a given meaning from any particular play, have been concerned rather to situate Ionesco's drama as a whole within the context of a living and developing climate of speculation. For French philosophy, under the influence of Bergson on the one hand and of the phenomenologists on the other, is far broader in scope than its English counterpart —in particular, the phenomenological movement has witnessed a constant interaction between "pure" litera-ture and abstract speculation, of a kind almost unknown in this country. Even during the few years since the war, three major literary movements—the Existentialists, the New Realists (or "*chosistes*," as their enemies call them) and the *avant-garde* theatre—have sprung directly from the teachings of men such as Husserl and Heidegger, Jean Wahl, and Merleau-Ponty, while Sartre contrives to combine in his own person the (to us) almost irreconcilable characters of philosopher, moralist, politician, and man of letters. Thus there is nothing far-fetched or esoteric about the attempt to translate, say, Ionesco's handling of *décor*, or his obsession with "proliferation" on the stage, in terms of the phenomenological "theory of perception," or to explain the psychological instability of his characters in terms of the suspected insufficiency of Aristotelian logic. To understand his relationship with the philosophers— even with the more-than-controversial Lupasco—is per-haps the only way to grasp the "meaning" of his plays; while at the same time, to experience the plays is in itself to grasp, in part at least, the meaning of the philosophers. Thus Vannier's remarkable analysis of the significance of Ionesco's treatment of language, or Doubrovsky's care-ful study of the exact attitude to formal logic revealed in Ionesco's humour, may count among the most significant contributions that criticism so far has had to make.

It is similarly far too early as yet to attempt to estimate Ionesco's influence on his contemporaries. All that is permissible is to point to the existence of a "school" in which his influence is paramount, and to suggest directions in which his innovations may be expected to lead.

In France, the dramatists of the present *avant-garde* form a compact and coherent group. Under the leadership of Ionesco and Beckett (and, to a far lesser degree, of Audiberti, whose early paradoxes in *Quoat-Quoat* and *Le Mal court* have since been watered down into a quasi-poetic slickness scarcely distinguishable from commercialism), are grouped Arthur Adamov, Jean Vauthier, Jean Genêt, Tardieu, Weingarten, and Arrabal, and the more lyrical Pichette and Schehadé. Of these, Jean Vauthier is perhaps the nearest in spirit to Ionesco; both *Le Personnage combattant* and *Les Prodiges* reveal the same terror of the encroaching world of inanimate objects, the same disdain for the sequences of logic, the same unfathomable pessimism—with this distinction, that there is very little humour in Vauthier, while at the same time, such poetry as there is, is less spontaneous and more conventional. Jean Genêt's *Les Bonnes* is a highly significant indication of the wealth of dramatic possibilities which may spring from the disintegration of classical psychology, while Fernando Arrabal (in *Le Cimetière des voitures*) brings to the drama a quality of imagination in no way inferior to Ionesco's, and at the same time, a powerful sense of injustice—a *ferocity*, which is lacking in Ionesco, and which may, in the end of things, deny him ultimate greatness.

Much of Arrabal, much even of Vauthier, is still immature and imitative; and the same applies to Ionesco's disciples of the English school—Ann Jellicoe, Nigel Dennis, and N. F. Simpson, among others. Harold Pinter alone, perhaps, has as yet achieved a real stature of his own, although the English tendency is always, at the last minute, to fight shy of the unexplained and to offer at least the shadow of a *reason*. At the Royal Court Theatre

in London, complains Towarnicki, there was a distinct
tendency to play *Les Chaises* as though it were Chekhov,
and at the Arts, also in London, *Le Nouveau Locataire*—
horribile dictu!—as though it were Brecht! "In England, it
was as though every character had to have a sort of
rational justification."[18] The junk and clutter of *The
Caretaker* is pure Ionesco; so also is the failure in communication, the desperate search for what can never be
achieved, the disintegration of language, the disintegration of psychology. But the key figure in *The Caretaker* is
Aston; and once it is stated that Aston spent part of his
life in a mental hospital, then nothing is surprising any
more. The anti-logic, the unexpected (after all!) was
nothing but a neat dramatic trick; now the "rational
justification" has been revealed, and all the teetering
universe returns to order and security. Perhaps it is only
N. F. Simpson, in *A Resounding Tinkle*, who really catches
an echo of Ionesco's cosmic lunacy—but at what a cost!
That which is not rational, insists the English mind (heed-
less of warnings), cannot be serious—and there stands *A
Resounding Tinkle* to prove the point: all the illogic, all the
chaos, all the shattering inconsequence—and *none of the
meaning*. Ionesco himself has confessed that he despises
Feydeau, for all the brilliance of his technique; for the
essence of the "tragic farce" is that it is first and foremost
tragic. Feydeau's is not; Labiche's is not; nor is Simpson's.
It is Ionesco with the stuffing taken out.

Yet obviously the full extent of a revolution cannot
be gauged, let alone absorbed and inwardly digested,
within the span of one decade. It is perhaps only now
that we are really beginning to perceive the implications
of Chekhov—and *La Cantatrice* may well be destined to
contain the seeds of the greatest dramatic overthrow
since *The Cherry Orchard*.[19] Moreover, Ionesco himself is
still searching for solutions, still grappling with the
problems of form. If *La Cantatrice*, *Les Chaises*, *La Leçon*,
Jacques, *Le Nouveau Locataire* are all but perfect in their

classical restraint and intensity, neither the full-length plays (*Amédée*, *Le Tueur*, *Rhinocéros*), nor the miniatures contained in the *Sept Petits Sketches* have finally come to terms with their own dimensions. None the less, and in spite of these hesitations and uncertainties, Ionesco has already given us—perhaps for the first time since Chekhov—the spectacle of a totally *serious* dramatist who is completely master of his own technique. He has given us a new attitude to dialogue, reducing it to the status of a running commentary on the action, yet at the same time imbuing it with a poetic power of incantation which, alone and unaided, has the force to bring his characters to life. He has shown us that a failure in communication—which is perhaps the very height of realism—can be a positive instead of a negative dramatic effect; and, at the same time, he has revealed that "naturalism" is not the old bogey, the implacable enemy of good theatre that every "new-look" dramatist from Toller onwards believed it to be, but that, reduced from the position of master to that of servant, it can be used and exploited whenever the play demands it. He has endowed the accessories of the theatre with life, giving them a new and active role in the unfolding of the drama, and correspondingly he has set the actor in a new perspective. He has integrated visual effect and rhythm into the play in such a way as to create what is in effect a new dramatic *genre*—a *genre* related to the ballet (*musique concrète* and all), yet potentially far more powerful, more disturbing, and of infinitely greater scope than ballet even at its best. He has realised the ambitions of Artaud on the one hand, of the Surrealists on the other. He has opened up a whole new world to the drama—a world where "reality" is not limited to the sensually verifiable or to the rationally possible, a world where the destruction of psychological probability does not entail the destruction of dramatic life. He has fashioned a new synthesis of the comic and the tragic, a new dramatic tension to replace the old and time-honoured machinations of "suspense." He has re-discovered the antique dramatic emotions of Pity and Terror (the "intolerable"), and softened their implicit cruelty with a veil of pathos which has never yet degenerated into sentimentality. Finally, he has evolved a drama supremely well-adapted to our world—that world in which science has escaped beyond the bounds of logic, in which the only "meaning" is that which takes account of absurdity, and the only reality that which includes the materially "impossible." He himself would claim that, by shattering the dictatorial dominion of "realism," he has "restored reality"; let us allow William Saroyan to take the paradox to its final form:

Up to the present, Beckett and Ionesco are the only *men of science* among the dramatists we have.[20]

REFERENCES

1. Lerminier, "Dialogue avec Ionesco," p. 51.
2. *Ibid.*
3. *Observer*, 13 Jul. 1958.
4. E.g. *Le Figaro*, 16 Oct. 1955, *Le Monde*, 13 Oct. 1955.
5. N.R.F., II. 31–2 (III. 126–9).
6. N.R.F., II. 56 (III. 149).
7. *Ibid.*
8. "Mes Critiques et moi," p. 3.
9. Marcel Brion, "Sur Ionesco," p. 273.
10. "Théâtre et anti-théâtre," p. 149.
11. William Saroyan, "Ionesco," p. 206.
12. Reported by Catherine Valogne, "Dialogue avec Ionesco . . . ," p. 8.
13. Marc Beigbeder, *"Comment s'en débarrasser . . . ,"* p. 66.
14. *Ibid.*
15. Pierre-Aimé Touchard, "Eugène Ionesco," pp. 91–102: "Un Nouveau Fabuliste," pp. 3–13; "Eugène Ionesco a réinventé les mythes du théâtre," p. 2.
16. Jacques Lemarchand, "Le Théâtre d'Eugène Ionesco," in N.R.F., I. 10–11.
17. Cp., however, Bibliography, arts. by Benmussa, Kempf, Lutembi, and Moussy.
18. Frédéric Towarnicki, "Ionesco des *Chaises* vides . . . ," p. 10.
19. Cp. Lawrence Kitchin, "Theatre, nothing but Theatre," p. 39.
20. Saroyan, "Ionesco," pp. 207–8.

BIBLIOGRAPHY

All editions cited in text or references are marked * in this bibliography. L.S. = Ionesco, *Théâtre*, Collection "Locus Solus," Vol. I; N.R.F. = Ionesco, *Théâtre*, Collection "N.R.F.," Vol. I or Vol. II; *Plays* = Ionesco, *Plays*, tr. Watson (Vols. I–III) and Prouse (Vol. IV); C.'P. = Cahiers du Collège de 'Pataphysique; C.S. = Cahiers des Saisons; C.R.-B. = Cahiers de la Compagnie Madeleine Renaud—Jean-Louis Barrault.

I. IONESCO'S WORKS

1. Plays

These are listed in chronological order of first performance, and the date of first performance is given in brackets after the title.

La Cantatrice chauve (1950) = *The Bald Prima-Donna.* C.'P., Nos. 7 (n.d.), pp. 11–19, and 8–9 (n.d.), pp. 59–68; L.S.; * N.R.F., 1; * *Plays*, 1.

La Leçon (1951) = *The Lesson.* L.S.; * N.R.F., 1; * *Plays*, 1.

Les Chaises (1952) = *The Chairs.* * N.R.F., 1; * *Plays*, 1.

Victimes du devoir (1953) = *Victims of Duty.* * N.R.F., 1; * *Plays*, 11.

Sept Petits Sketches (1953), including: (i) *Les Grandes Chaleurs*, d'après Caragiale (MS. now lost); (ii) *La Jeune Fille à marier* = *Maid to Marry* (*Lettres Nouvelles*, Jun. 1953; * N.R.F., 11; * *Plays*, 111); (iii) *Les connaissez-vous?* (MS. now lost); (iv) *Le Maître* = *The Leader* (*Bizarre*, No. 1, May 1955, pp. 3–11; * N.R.F., 11; * *Plays*, 1V), of which an operatic version with music by Germaine Tailleferre was broadcast Jul. 1960; (v) *La Nièce-épouse* (exists only in MS.); (vi) *Le Rhume onirique* (MS. now lost); and (vii) *Le Salon de l'automobile* (first produced as a radio-play 1951; * L.S.).

Amédée ou Comment s'en débarrasser (1954) = *Amédée or How to Get Rid of It.* Originally published as a short story, "Oriflamme," in *Nouvelle N.R.F.*, No. 14 (1 Feb. 1954), pp. 203–13. As play, * N.R.F., 1; * *Plays*, 11.

Jacques ou La Soumission (1955) = *Jacques or Obedience.* L.S.; * N.R.F., 1; * *Plays*, 1.

Le Tableau (1955). * C.'P., n.s., dossiers 1–2 (n.d.), pp. 5–56.

L'Impromptu de l'Alma, ou Le Caméléon du berger (1956) = *Improvisation, or The Shepherd's Chameleon.* * N.R.F., 11; * *Plays*, 111.

L'Avenir est dans les œufs, ou Il faut de tout pour faire un monde (1957) = *The Future is in Eggs, or It takes all Sorts to make a World.* C.'P., No. 19 (n.d.), pp. 15–30; * N.R.F., 11; * *Plays*, 1V.

Le Nouveau Locataire (1957: previously performed in Finland and in England) = *The New Tenant*. * N.R.F., II; * *Plays*, II.

Tueur sans gages (1959) = *The Killer*. First published as a short story, "La Photo du colonel," in *Nouvelle N.R.F.*, No. 35 (1 Nov. 1955), pp. 890–904. As play, * N.R.F., II; * *Plays*, III.

Le Rhinocéros (1960) = *Rhinoceros*. First published as a short story, "Rhinocéros," in *Les Lettres nouvelles*, No. 52 (Sep. 1957). As play, in Collection "Le Manteau d'Arlequin," * Paris (Gallimard) 1959; * *Plays*, IV.

Apprendre à marcher (1960). Ballet, choreography by Deryk Mendel; performed by Ballets Modernes de Paris (Françoise et Dominique). Scenario only in * MS.

Scène à quatre (1960, Spoleto International Festival) = *Foursome*. C.'P., n.s., No. 7 (n.d.), pp. 65–72. Tr. Donald M. Allen in * *Evergreen Review*, IV. 13 (May–Jun. 1960), pp. 46–53.

Les Salutations (not yet performed). * *Les Lettres françaises*, No. 805 (31 Dec. 1959).

2. Collected Editions of Plays

Théâtre, in Collection "Locus Solus," Vol. I (here cited as L.S.), Paris (Arcanes) 1953.

Théâtre, in Collection "N.R.F.," (here cited as N.R.F.), Vols I and II, Paris (Gallimard) 1954 and 1958.

Plays, (here cited as *Plays*), tr. Donald Watson (Vols. I–III) and Derek Prouse (Vol. IV), London (Calder) 1958 (Vols. I–II) and 1960 (Vols. III–IV). Vols. II–IV of this edition have also been published in the U.S.A., by Grove Press, under the following titles: *Amédée, The New Tenant, Victims of Duty*, tr. Donald Watson (=*Plays*, II), N.Y. 1958; *The Killer and other Plays (Improvisation, or The Shepherd's Chameleon; Maid to Marry)* tr. Donald Watson (=*Plays*, III), N.Y. 1960; *Rhinoceros and other Plays (The Leader, The Future is in Eggs)*, tr. Derek Prouse (=*Plays*, IV), N.Y. 1960. In place of *Plays*, I, Grove Press have also published *Four Plays (The Bald Soprano; The Lesson; Jack, or The Submission)*, tr. Donald M. Allen, N.Y. 1958.

3. Critical Articles, Interviews, etc.

"Caragiale: 1852–1912," in *Les Ecrivains célèbres*, Vol. III, Paris (Mazenod) 1953, pp. 218–19.

"L'Invraisemblable, l'insolite, mon univers"; in * *Arts*, No. 424 (14/20 Aug. 1953), pp. 1–2. Repr. in C.S., No. 15 (Winter 1959), under title "Je n'ai jamais réussi. . . ."

"Point de départ"; in C.S., No. 1 (Aug. 1955). Repr. under title "Essays: (i) Point of Departure" (tr. Leonard C. Pronko) in * *Theatre Arts* (N.Y.), June 1958, pp. 17–18; also in *Plays*, I.

"Mes Pièces ne prétendent pas sauver le monde"; in *Express*, 15/16 Oct. 1955, p. 8.

"Pour Cocteau," in C.S., No. 2 (Oct. 1955).

"Théâtre et anti-théâtre," in * C.S., No. 2 (Oct. 1955), pp. 149–151. Repr. under title "Essays: (ii) Theatre and Anti-Theatre" (tr. Leonard C. Pronko), in *Theatre Arts* (N.Y.), June 1958, pp. 18, 77.

"Mes Critiques et moi,"; in *Arts*, No. 556 (22/28 Feb. 1956), p. 3.

"Finalement, je suis pour le classicisme," in *Bref*, No. 11 (15 Feb. 1956), pp. 1–2.

"The World of Eugène Ionesco," in *International Theatre Annual*, No. 2, ed. Harold Hobson, London (Calder) 1957. Repr. in * *Tulane Drama Review*, III. 1 (Oct. 1958), pp. 46–8.

"Dans les armes de la ville," in C.R.-B., No. 20 (Oct. 1957), pp. 3–5.

"L'Avant-garde n'existe pas au théâtre"; in *Arts*, No. 651 (1/7 Jan. 1958), p. 6.

"Qu'est-ce que l'avant-garde en 1958?" in * *Les Lettres françaises*, No. 717 (10/17 Apr. 1958), p. 1. Repr. in C.S., No. 15 (Winter 1959), p. 209–11, under title "Lorsque j'écris. . . ."

"Expérience du théâtre," in *Nouvelle N.R.F.*, No. 62 (1958), pp. 247–270; repr. under title "Discovering the Theatre," tr. Leonard C. Pronko, in * *Tulane Drama Review*, IV. 1 (Sep. 1959), pp. 3–18.

"Ni un dieu, ni un démon," in C.R.-B., Nos. 22/23 (May 1958), pp. 130–34.

"Reality in Depth," (part of an address given by Ionesco at the Institut Français de Londres) in *Encore*, V. 1 (May–Jun. 1958), pp. 9–10.

"The Playwright's Role," in the *Observer*, 29 Jun. 1958, Repr. (in Fr.) in *Express*, 17 Jul. 1958; under title * "Ionesco à l'heure anglaise," in * *Théâtre populaire*, No. 34 (1959), pp. 132–4; under title, "Controverse londonienne," in C.S., No. 15 (Winter 1959). See also below under "Le Cœur n'est pas sur la main," and II. GENERAL CRITICISM, under TYNAN.

"La Tragédie du langage: Comment un manuel pour apprendre l'anglais est devenu ma première pièce," in *Spectacles*, No. 2 (Jul. 1958), pp. 2–5.

"Le Cœur n'est pas sur la main," (written for the *Observer*, but not published by that paper), in C.S., No. 15 (Winter 1959), pp. 262–7.

"Naissance de *La Cantatrice*," in C.S., No. 15 (Winter 1959), pp. 282–284.

"La Démystification par l'humour noir"; in *L'Avant-Scène*, No. 191 (15 Feb. 1959: "numéro spécial présenté par Eugène Ionesco"), pp. 5–6.

"Celui qui ose ne pas haïr devient un traître," in *Arts*, No. 711 (3 Mar. 1959), pp. 1–2.

"Eugène Ionesco ouvre le feu," (textual report of Ionesco's opening address to the Eighth Congress of the International Theatre Institute, Helsinki, Jun. 1959), in *Théâtre dans le monde*, VIII (Autumn 1959), pp. 171–202.

"Depuis dix ans, je me bats contre l'esprit bourgeois et les tyrannies politiques," in *Arts*, No. 758 (20/26 Jan. 1960), p. 5.

"Interview du Transcendant Satrape Ionesco par lui-même," in *C.'P.*, n.s., dossiers 10–11 (n.d.), pp. 181–2. Repr. in *L'Observateur littéraire (France-Observateur)*, 21 Jan. 1960, p. 21.

"Le Bloc-notes d'Eugène Ionesco," in *Arts*, No. 763 (24 Feb. 1960), p. 2.

"Printemps 1939: les débris du souvenir. Pages de journal," in *C.R.-B.*, No. 29 (Feb. 1960), pp. 96–114.

"Pages de Journal," in *Nouvelle N.R.F.*, No. 86 (1 Feb. 1960), pp. 220–33.

"Entretien avec Eugène Ionesco," in *Cahiers libres de la Jeunesse*, No. 2 (15 Mar. 1960), pp. 12–13.

4. Translation

DAN, PAVEL: *Le Père Urcan*. Tr. Gabrielle Cabrini and Eugène Ionesco. With preface by Ionesco, pp. 7–18. Marseilles (Jean Vignaud) 1945.

II. GENERAL CRITICISM (SELECTED)

[ANON]: "Auto-Interview: Que faut-il penser de la nouvelle pièce d'Eugène Ionesco, *Tueurs* [*sic*] *sans Gages?* Ionesco répond à Eugène," in *Express*, 29 Feb. 1959.

ABIRACHED, ROBERT: "Ionesco et *Les Chaises*," in *Les Études*, CCXC (Jul.–Sep. 1956), pp. 116–20.

BASTIEN, HERMAS: "Erotisme et technique," (a study of *Le Salon de l'automobile*), in *Médecine et hygiène*, 10 Apr. 1960.

BEIGBEDER, MARC: "Comment s'en Débarrasser, d'Eugène Ionesco," in *Théâtre de France*, Vol. IV, Paris (Les Publications de France) 1955, p. 66.

——: *Le Théâtre en France depuis la libération*, Paris (Bordas) 1959.

BENMUSSA, SIMONE: "Les Ensevelis dans le théâtre d'Eugène Ionesco," in *C.R.-B.*, Nos. 22/23 (May 1958), pp. 197–207.

BONZON, PHILIPPE: "Molière ou le Complexe de Ionesco," in *Perspectives du Théâtre*, No. 2 (Feb. 1960), pp. 7–10.

BOSQUET, ALAIN: "Comment se débarrasser du personnage," in *C.S.*, No. 15 (Winter 1959), pp. 242–4.

——: "Le Théâtre d'Eugène Ionesco, ou les trente-six recettes du comique," in *Combat*, 17 Feb. 1955.

——: "Le Théâtre en ébullition d'Eugène Ionesco," in *Combat*, 27 Nov. 1958.

BRION, MARCEL: "Sur Ionesco," in *Mercure de France*, No. 1150 (Jun. 1959), pp. 272–277.

CAHIERS DE LA COMPAGNIE MADELEINE RENAUD—JEAN-LOUIS BARRAULT, No. 29 (Feb. 1960: special issue devoted to Ionesco).

CAHIERS DES SAISONS, No. 15 (Winter 1959: special issue devoted to Ionesco).

DAMIENS, CLAUDE: "Eugène Ionesco, ou le Comique de l'Absurde," in *Paris-Théâtre*, No. 156 (1960), pp. 2–3.

DOUBROVSKY, J. S.: "Ionesco and the Comedy of the Absurd," in *Yale French Studies*, No. 23 (Summer 1959), pp. 3–10. Repr. under title "Le Rire d'Eugène Ionesco," in *Nouvelle N.R.F.*, No. 86 (1 Feb. 1960), pp. 313–23.

FRANCUEIL, BERNARD: "Digression automobile & dilectus quemadmodum Filius unicornium," in *C.'P.*, n.s., dossiers 10–11 (n.d.), pp. 172–80.

GIRARD, DENIS: "L'Anti-Théâtre d'Eugène Ionesco," in *Modern Languages*, XL. 2 (Jun. 1959), pp. 45–52.

GOUHIER, HENRI: "Eugène Ionesco," in *La Table ronde*, No. 137 (May 1959), pp. 176–80.

——: "Un Théâtre humain de la cruauté," in *La Table ronde*, No. 147 (Mar. 1960), pp. 178–81.

HUMEAU, EDMOND: "Eugène Ionesco, ou le théâtre de la contradiction," in *Preuves*, No. 32 (Oct. 1953), pp. 84–6.

KANTERS, ROBERT: "Entretien avec Ionesco," in *Express*, 28 Jan. 1960, pp. 36–7.

KEMPF, ROGER: "L'Homme et la femme dans l'espace d'Eugène Ionesco," in *Romanische Forschungen*, LXXII. 1/2 (1960), pp. 95–8.

KITCHIN, LAWRENCE: "Theatre, nothing but Theatre," in *Encounter*, No. 55 (Apr. 1958), pp. 39–42.

KNOWLES, DOROTHY: "Ionesco's Rhinoceroses," in *Drama*, Autumn 1960, pp. 35–9.

LAUBREAUX, RAYMOND: "Situation de Ionesco," in *Théâtre d'aujourd'hui*, Jan.–Feb. 1959, pp. 42–5.

LEMARCHAND, JACQUES: "Les Débuts d'Ionesco," in *C.S.*, No. 15 (Winter 1959), pp. 215–18.

——: "Spectacles Ionesco," in *Nouvelle N.R.F.*, No. 36 (1 Dec. 1955), pp. 1148–53.

LERMINIER, GEORGES: "Clés pour Ionesco," in *Théâtre d'aujourd'hui*, No. 3 (Sep.–Oct. 1957), pp. 3–5.

——: "Dialogue avec Ionesco," in *Pensée française*, No. 6 (Jun. 1959), pp. 51–3.

LUTEMBI: "Contribution à une étude de *La Cantatrice chauve*," in *C.'P.*, Nos. 8–9 (n.d.), pp. 87–9.

ꟼora, Edith: "Ionesco: 'Le Rire? L'Aboutissement d'un drame!'," in *Nouvelles litteraires*, No. 1686 (24 Dec. 1959).

ꟼoussy, Marcel: "De Victor à Jacques, ou de la révolte à la soumission," in C.R.-B., No. 29 (Feb. 1960), pp. 27–8.

ꟼuller, André: "Techniques de l'avant-garde," in *Théâtre populaire*, No. 18 (1 May 1956), pp. 21–9.

Quatrezoneilles: "*La Leçon* par Eugène Ionesco," in C.'P., Nos. 8–9 (n.d.), pp. 99–100.

ꟼobbe-Grillet, Alain: "Eugène Ionesco," in *Critique*, No. 73, Jun. 1953, pp. 564–5.

ꟼarisson, Paul: "*Tueur sans Gages*," in *Aux Ecoutes*, 16 Jan. 1959.

ꟼaroyan, William: "Ionesco," in *Theatre Arts* (N.Y.), Jul. 1958. Repr. in * C.S., No. 15 (Winter 1959), pp. 206–8.

ꟼaurel, Renée: "Saint Ionesco, l'Anti-Brecht," in *Temps modernes*, No. 158 (1959), pp. 1656–61.

ꟼchérer, Jacques: "L'Evolution de Ionesco," in *Lettres nouvelles*, n.s., No. 1, (Mar.–Apr. 1960), pp. 91–6.

ꟼelz, Jean: "L'Homme encombré d'Ionesco," in *Lettres nouvelles*, No. 53 (Oct. 1957), pp. 477–82.

——: "Un Nouveau Ionesco," in *Lettres nouvelles*, n.s., No. 1 (4 Mar. 1959), pp. 32–3.

ꟼouchard, Pierre-Aimé: "Eugène Ionesco," in *Revue de Paris*, Jul. 1960, pp. 91–102.

——: "Un Nouveau Fabuliste," in C.R.-B., No. 29 (Feb. 1960), pp. 3–13.

——: "Eugène Ionesco a réinventé les mythes du théâtre," in *Arts*, No. 608 (27 Feb./5 Mar. 1957), p. 2. Repr. under title: "La Loi du Théâtre," in C.S., No. 15 (Winter 1959), pp. 221–6.

ꟼowarnicki, Frédéric: "Ionesco des *Chaises* vides . . . à Broadway," in *Spectacles*, No. 2 (Jul. 1958), pp. 6–12.

ꟼynan, Kenneth; Orson Welles; Philip Toynbee; Eugène Ionesco; and Others: articles first printed in the *Observer*, 22 and 29 Jun., 6 and 13 Jul., 1958. Repr. under title "Ionesco à l'heure anglaise," in *Théâtre populaire*, No. 34 (1959), pp. 129–41; in *Express*, 17 Jul. 1958; and under title "Controverse londonienne," in C.S., No. 15 (Winter 1959), pp. 255–267. See above, I. 3, under "Le Cœur n'est pas dans la main."

ꟼalogne, Catherine: "Dialogue avec Ionesco sur Ionesco et *Le Rhinocéros*," in *Lettres françaises*, No. 808 (21–7 Jan. 1960), pp. 1, 8.

ꟼannier, Jean: "Langages de l'avant-garde," in *Théâtre populaire*, No. 18 (1 May 1956), pp. 30–9.

ꟼatson, Donald: "The Plays of Eugène Ionesco," in *Tulane Drama Review*, III. 1 (Oct. 1958), pp. 48–53.

III. BIBLIOGRAPHY

Partial Bibliographies are given in articles listed above, II, un[der]
GIRARD and LAUBREAUX. The main source hitherto has been th[e]
regular bibliographical supplement to the *Revue d'histoire du thé[âtre]*
but the author has compiled an interim bibliography (1950-[6]0)
which, together with a bibliography of articles in German concern[ing]
Ionesco, by Hans Rudolf Stauffacher, will in due course appea[r in]
the *Proceedings of the Leeds Philosophical and Literary Society*.

IV. MISCELLANEOUS

ARTAUD, ANTONIN: *Le Théâtre et son double*, Paris (Gallimard) 1[938].
    Tr. Mary C. Richards, * *The Theatre and its Double*, N.Y. (Gr[ove]
    Press) 1958.

CARAGIALE, ION-LUCA: *Théâtre choisi*, ed. Iosifesco, 2 vols., Buchar[est]
    1953.

LUPASCO, STÉPHANE: *Logique et contradiction*, Paris (P.U.F.) 1947.

URMUZ [DEMETRU DEMETRESCU-BUZAU]: Collected Works, ed[.]
    Sasa Pana, Bucharest (Collection Unu) 1930.

[VARIOUS]: "What is 'Pataphysics?" in *Evergreen Review*, No. [13,]
    N.Y. (Grove Press) 1960.